ROTARY SWING GOLF

The Anatomy of the Golf Swing

Instructor Certification Manual

Level 1

First Edition

Chuck Quinton

With Al Consoli

FIRST EDITION

TABLE OF CONTENTS

Foreword

The golf swing is one of the most complex athletic movements in all of sports due to the precision required for successful ball striking. From a teacher's perspective, it can be almost an enigma watching a golfer with a terrible looking golf swing hit the ball with power and control while a golfer with a beautiful swing struggles to get the ball airborne. How does this happen, and how do you teach these two students to improve? One instructor will have the student do one thing, and another instructor will say the exact opposite. Is there not a set of fundamentals in golf that everyone should use to learn to swing the club? After all, there are fundamentals in everything else we learn in life. Imagine picking up a saxophone for the first time and going to get lessons. There is a specific way the instructor would show you how to hold the instrument, how to blow, how to hold your posture, how to push the keys, etc. And, if you went to see another instructor, they'd tell you basically the exactly same thing. However, with the most complex and precise motion in all of sport, you can rarely find two instructors that agree on anything, much less a common set of fundamentals. Why?

The answer is actually quite simple. Golf instruction has never been looked at exclusively from an anatomic or scientific perspective. Many golf instructors, like a herd of wildebeests running off a cliff, watch and blindly follow the top player of the era or their "favorite" swing on tour and teach the golf swing based on how that player appears to swing the club. How foolish is this? Common sense should tell you that there are a million ways to successfully strike a golf ball, but would you go and teach someone how to swing like Colin Montgomerie just because you liked his swing? What about Jim Furyk? No one on the PGA Tour has a more consistent path into impact that is more square through the hitting area than Furyk, according to Trackman data. Shouldn't we then teach everyone to swing like Furyk?

The truth is we as instructors shouldn't teach students how to swing exactly like anyone presently on the PGA Tour because no one swings 100% anatomically correctly – yet. Tiger Woods is admittedly the closest and continues to get closer. As of this writing, he has altered his setup during the 2009 season to be less on the balls of his feet, which as you will learn, will protect his hip, knee and back during the rest of his career. But the truth of the matter is that even Tiger is not perfect because he has either chosen to ignore the anatomical absolutes of the body or simply isn't aware of the scientific evidence underlying what you are about to learn. I'm quite certain it's the latter as Tiger won't be able to deny or argue what you are about to read on the following pages because it isn't based on opinion or preference, but medical and scientific fact.

For once, you are about to learn that there are indeed a set of fundamentals in the golf swing, and for once, you and your students will actually be rewarded for working on your golf swings rather than ending up worse off than you started. We hope you enjoy the process of discovery and learning and share it with all your students as they will be the greatest benefactors of your Level 1 Rotary Swing Tour Instructor Certification. Golf will be fun again, and you will understand the golf swing like you never have before when finished with this course.

Chuck Quinton

Rotary Swing Founder

Introduction

While this manual is directed toward golf instruction professionals, the lay person will likely find it extremely helpful as well. Some of the terminology is technical but well established in the medical field, so for the sake of consistency, we use the medical terms where appropriate. There is a glossary in the back of the book if you come across a term that is unfamiliar. By the same token, some of the terms have been simplified to make it more clear to the student what the goal of the movement is. For instance, when we refer to the hands moving in a vertical plane in front of the body during the backswing, the correct technical term would be "shoulder flexion". However, we are using the term "shoulder elevation" to paint the picture that the arms/hands are being "elevated" by the muscles in the shoulders.

Because the vast majority of golfers in the world are right handed, the book is written in a way that exclusively references the right-handed player. This is done to avoid the cumbersome terminology of "trailing hand," "target side hip", etc. If you play left-handed, you will need to simply transpose left and right.

This manual is written first and foremost to educate the instructor on how to teach the Rotary Swing Tour (RST), which is an objective approach to the golf swing based on anatomy, research and physics rather than personal preference, bias or how the top golfers in the world swing the club. It is designed to help anyone wanting to learn how to become a great teacher develop a sound understanding of the true core components of the swing. Because there is a lot of material to cover just on how the body moves, there is little discussion on topics such as swing plane, ball flight control, etc. These are reserved for Level 2 and Master RST Certification. A strong base of knowledge is required before ever worrying about those topics, and that strong base is provided both here in the Level 1 certification manual as well as the videos on the website at www.RotarySwing.com. Regarding the website videos, there are some things that are much more easily explained in motion rather than print. Many topics are omitted from this manual or only touched on lightly because they are much more easily explained in the videos on the website. If you feel a topic hasn't been covered enough detail here, it very likely has been online, so check the website. It is updated each month with new videos and there is more than 18 hours of content on there already.

If you are reading this manual to become RST Level 1 Certified, you should be aware that the 130 plus test questions on the exam are taken both from this manual and from the videos on the website. Anything published under the RST section of the website is fair game in the exam, and you should be fully prepared to answer questions from both. At the time of this First Edition writing, a minimum passing score of 90% is required to attain Level 1 certification. This is subject to change, but if anything, the minimum passing score will move higher, not lower. We want to ensure that the RST Certified Instructors are, quite literally, the most knowledgeable, helpful and well-respected instructors in the industry and will do whatever is necessary to protect that reputation. Your investment in RST Certification will be one that will carry a high price tag for entry in terms of study required but will bring with it the respect reserved for the brightest experts in the golf world.

Good luck!

Chapter 1: What Is a Fundamental?

Given the complexity of the movements of the golf swing and the precision required for success, it would seem evident the need for a clearly defined and established set of fundamentals from which to learn. Most everything else we've learned in life was based on some industry-wide accepted set of fundamentals. When learning to play a musical instrument, we never feared that if we took a lesson from someone other than our normal instructor that he or she might teach us something completely different or even opposite from our previous instructor. When learning to drive a car, there were a common set of fundamentals. If you learned how to drive a stick shift, you were taught to slowly ease out the clutch while gently pressing in the accelerator. I doubt that anyone tried to teach you to slowly let out the gas while gently pushing in the clutch! However, you can take ten different golf lessons from ten different instructors and be taught ten different things. How on earth could anyone learn this way?

Well, history has proven they can't. It's a well known fact that golfers' handicaps haven't changed much over the last 50 years, and I believe that instruction is at the root of this trend. The most significant problem with golf instruction since its inception is the fact that it has never been taught on a common set of fundamentals for the simple reason that no one seems to be able to agree on any. This is to be expected given how each instructor has come up with his own "fundamentals" that he teaches. Most instruction material published in the past has been based on how the top player of that era swings the golf club. That's it. No underlying explanation for why or how, just "this works for me so you should do it to." When Bobby Jones was the greatest golfer in the world, everyone wanted to learn to swing like

Jones. When Ben Hogan became the next world beater, he became the most sought after swing guru and published a book that is still a favorite amongst golfers today. But then a young kid named Jack Nicklaus came along and swung the club and arms in a much more upright fashion with a massive leg drive. All of a sudden, Hogan's more flattish swing plane was no longer in vogue. Today, of course, like lost puppy dogs trying to find someone to feed them, countless instructors will put your swing up next to Tiger Woods and say "Here's what Tiger does, and here's what you do. Don't what Tiger does." They do this all while having little to no understanding of the biomechanics of Tiger's swing, including the faulty movement and setup patterns that have caused him injury. It won't be long before Tiger's swing is overtaken by someone else who hits it longer and straighter, and that golfer's movements form the basis for the next "model swing."

If this seems insane to you--changing the core of what golf instructors teach based on who's the top dog at the moment--that's because it is. At some point, it just makes sense to ignore how all the golfers on the PGA Tour swing and take a completely objective look at human anatomy, physics and human physiology and say "How is the body designed to accomplish the task of striking the golf ball safely, powerfully and efficiently, and how can the brain learn this new movement pattern?" If that makes sense to you, then the Rotary Swing Tour will make sense to you because that's exactly what we did. Rather than define a set of fundamentals based on our own biases or preferences of golfer's swings that we liked or instructional advice we felt made "good tips", we decided to put together a set of fundamentals based on the very definition of the word. According to Webster's Dictionary, a *fundamental* is:

a: serving as an original or generating source
b : serving as a basis supporting existence or determining essential structure or function
c: of central importance
d: of or relating to essential structure, function

When determining what a fundamental of the RST golf swing is, it must first meet these criteria. To make things simple, below is a list of synonyms and antonyms to memorize:

- *Synonyms of "Fundamental"*

    - **Primary**

    - **Origin**

    - **Central**

    - **Absolute**

- *Antonyms of "Fundamental"*

    - **Secondary**

    - **Consequential**

    - **Peripheral**

    - **Dependent**

So, from this point forward, anything that is truly a fundamental of the golf swing should stand the test of being primary, origin, central and absolute. If it does not, then by its very definition, it can't be a fundamental.

Exercise

List 5 fundamentals of the golf swing that meet the above criteria.

1.

2.

3.

4.

5.

It's likely that you'll find it difficult to do so, especially if someone challenges you to defend your answers. For instance, let's take swing plane. To many instructors swing plane is all the matters. They are unconcerned with how the body moves, focusing only on the arms and hands and how they create a swing plane. However, swing plane can NOT be a fundamental of the golf swing according to the definition of the word because it is completely DEPENDENT on the movements of the body, arms and hands. It is SECONDARY to these movements and DEPENDENT on how the muscles in the body fire and happens in the PERIPHARY of what is central to the golf swing – the movements of the body. If you'll notice, swing plane fits perfectly with all the antonyms of what a fundamental is. We're not saying swing plane is not important, but it cannot, by definition, be a fundamental.

In your quest to understand the truths about the golf swing, defining what a fundamental is and is not will take you a very long way toward finding what truly is important in the golf swing. If we revisit our swing plane example above, you will find that understanding how to correctly rotate the torso, perform shoulder elevation and right elbow flexion will create a swing plane. The club, by itself can do nothing, the muscles of the body moving the bones at their respective joints are what create the appearance of a swing plane, and therefore, each movement individually can be looked at as a fundamental as they are the ORIGIN of movement.

For some, the swing plane example may be too complex to understand at first, so let's take an easier one: stance width. Think to yourself what you have been told regarding stance width or perhaps what you have even taught your students. The most common advice is that the feet should be shoulder width apart. When I hear this, the first thing I do is ask that instructor, "Where are my legs attached, my shoulders or my hips?" Of course, they answer the hips. So my next question is, "What does the width of my shoulders have to do with the width of my stance?" There is NO direct correlation between the two. Some golfers have very broad shoulders and very narrow hips and vice versa. This useless piece of advice is not only vague but not based on anything central or absolute. And worse yet, the instructor can't provide an answer as to "why" he wants me to do it, and that is unacceptable. Everything you do in the golf swing should have a very clear answer as to WHY it needs to be done that way and HOW to go about doing it. With RST, there is a very clear answer as to why, either based on anatomy, swing mechanics, physics or the physiology of the learning process and a very clear pathway on how to go about doing it.

For RST Instructors, the width of the stance is a fundamental that abides by the laws of "why" and "how." First, it is determined by the width of the pelvis since that is what determines neutral joint alignment (NJA), which is vital for power and injury prevention. Second, it is determined by the fundamental in the swing of weight transfer, which is inherent in all throwing and hitting athletic movements as it creates momentum that is again, necessary for maximum power. Third, while transferring the weight, we need the head to stay centered to make clean contact more consistently. A clean strike becomes increasingly difficult with our heads moving all over the place. Finally, it is based on the need to have the left hip in neutral at impact for safe and efficient rotation. Because of these requirements, the stance width for RST is 2 inches outside of neutral. This is the type of analytical thought process that goes into understanding each piece of the RST.

The point of this chapter is for you to understand that you should question absolutely everything you've heard about the golf swing in the past and everything you hear in the future. Anytime someone gives you a piece of swing advice, see if it qualifies as a fundamental and ask them the all important question, "Why?" Why is a very scary question for many golf instructors because they don't have a clue why. They were either taught to do it that way by another instructor, read about it in a golf instruction book or found it to work in their own swing that is very likely built around a chain of compensations. In all probability, they will have no irrefutable answer for why they want someone to move the way they are asking. If they can't answer why, then you should very seriously reconsider who you're taking lessons with and how their lack of knowledge may be putting you at serious risk for injury. If you, the instructor, want to have the answer to "why" going forward, you've come to the right place.

Chapter 2: How the Brain Learns

Before we can begin to dissect the golf swing, we must first understand, as teachers, how the brain learns. The brain is not engineered to learn at 100 mph. For example the first time you climbed into a car to learn how to drive, your instructor did not tell you to hop on the open highway and "Floor it!" You first learned where all the controls were, what the pedals did and all the other fundamentals of how the automobile works. You would most likely step on the gas for the first time in a parking lot or on a backcountry road. This safe environment with minimal distractions would allow you to slowly get acclimatized to the vehicle and to learn the fundamentals of its operation. You would learn how the gas works, how the breaks work, then the steering wheel, then the gear selector and so on. And, you would learn each of these one at a time. In other words, you would take in small pieces of information that your brain could easily digest and then move onto the next bit of information. Mastering operation of the car would be ingrained by repetition through practice with constant and immediate correction. If you've ever taught someone how to drive a car, you know just how overwhelming this process can be to the student for the first time. But, by guiding them slowly, piece by piece, they learn each fundamental as you guide them through the process. In this manner you or the person you are teaching systematically learned how to operate the vehicle.

As this information is processed by the brain and you continue to repeat the necessary tasks to operate the vehicle, you begin to feel more comfortable that you would be able to competently operate the vehicle at higher rates of speed and in an environment with more distractions. We're not quite ready for the 405 at rush hour, but we're systematically working up to it. In other words, the more pieces of information you learn to perform without having to think about it, the more you are able to take on greater responsibility and stack more information on top of what you have previously learned. Eventually, you're able to perform numerous functions in order to operate the vehicle safely without giving it much thought, although clearly driving and talking on a cell phone are still too many tasks for most to be done safely.

If we take a moment to think about this logically, the golf swing should be learned in the same manner as how we learned to drive. Much in the same way that we learned each fundamental individually and then stacked another one on top of it, we will do the same in building our golf swing. It makes no sense for us to worry about the downswing if we cannot set up correctly to the golf ball. Once we observe a breakdown in a step, we must remove a piece and go back to perfect the previous step. Ben Hogan figured this process out many years ago and stated his position very eloquently:

> *"You simply cannot bypass the fundamentals in golf any more than you can sit down at a piano without a lesson and rip off the score of "My Fair Lady". Learning the grip, stance, and posture clearly and well is, in a way, like having to play the scales when learning piano. The best way to learn golf is a great deal like learning to play the piano: you practice a few things daily, you arrive at a solid foundation, and then you go on to practice a few more advanced things daily, continually increasing your skill."*

The point of Mr. Hogan's quote is simply this: learning is a systematic process and can only be successfully achieved through proper practice and repetition.

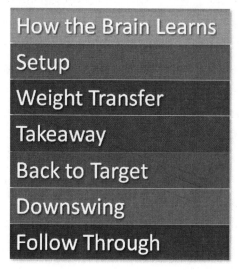

Figure 1 - The Rotary Swing Hierarchy of Learning.

The Rotary Swing model takes all of this into account and is built around a hierarchy for learning the golf swing. It contains the elements of a sound, biomechanically correct Rotary Golf Swing in the sequence that they must be learned. Each segment of this hierarchy will be covered in great detail in the following chapters.

Neuromuscular Re-education

Neuromuscular re-education is the definition given to any form of athletic training, rehabilitation program or bodily movement that requires muscles and nerves to relearn a certain behavior or specific sequence of movements. It is important for us to fully understand how our muscles and nerves eventually learn and develop the neural networks and pathways necessary to perform a task effectively and efficiently. As a new movement is introduced, the body begins to develop a broad kinesthetic sense (sensation of muscle movements through nerves) necessary to facilitate the movement (Dr. Larry van Such, http://www.athleticquickness.com/page.asp?page_id=53). As the first movement is perfected, the next segment is stacked on top of that movement. This forces the muscles and nerves to increase their kinesthetic ability or awareness to adapt to the new movement. The process is repeated, and ultimately, the muscles and nerves become perfectly coordinated together producing the desired effect. Every day one practices, the brain is constantly refining the pathways necessary to master these movements. This makes the movements appear effortless and without any conscious thought. When one masters a new motor skill, the athletic movement transitions from active effort to automatic ability. Essentially, the new movement pattern becomes hardwired into the brain. This is known as implicit or procedural memory.

It seems that as a motor skill enters the implicit memory, the neural pathways responsible for performing the task shift from one region in the brain to another. For example, in one experiment magnetic pulses were used to trigger neurons firing in the motor cortex in order to study neuronal activity during skill learning. During the practice time, while the subjects were learning the skill, the regions of neurons recruited got bigger, and the intensity of firing increased. Once the skill was mastered, the region shrank to original size again. Apparently a different region of the brain, probably the basal ganglia or cerebellum took over once the task became automatic (http://www.brainskills.co.uk/LearningMotorSkills.html). Let us examine this in greater detail to further understand this process. Scanning studies show that a person uses the frontal lobe, motor cortex and cerebellum while learning a new physical skill. Learning a motor skill involves following a set of procedures and can be eventually carried out largely without conscious attention. In fact, too much conscious attention directed to a motor skill while performing it can diminish the quality of its execution. When first learning the skill, attention and awareness are obviously required. The frontal lobe is engaged because working memory is needed, and the motor cortex of the cerebrum interacts with the cerebellum to control muscle movement. As practice continues, the activated areas of the motor cortex become larger as nearby neurons are recruited into the new skill network. However, the memory of the skill is not established until after practice stops. It takes about four to twelve hours for this consolidation to take place in the cerebellum, and most of it occurs during deep sleep. Once the skill is mastered, brain activity shifts to the cerebellum, which organizes and coordinates the movements and the timing to perform the task. Procedural memory is the mechanism, and the brain no longer needs to use its higher-order processes as the performance of the skill becomes automatic. Continued practice of the skill changes the brain structurally. These skills become so much part of the individual that they are difficult to change later in life (David A. Sousa, http://www.sagepub.com/upm-data/12749_Sousa_Chapter_1.pdf)

An effective example of this process is the movie *The Karate Kid*. In the movie, the teacher asked the student to perform numerous repetitions of a particular movement, all the while using very simple keywords that he kept repeating aloud while the motion was performed. After a day's worth of repetitions and hearing the key words for one particular movement, a new movement was introduced the following day with a new set of keywords. This continued for several days. On the final day, the teacher engages the student in sparring and simply shouts out the key words of the particular motion he wants the student to perform. Without even thinking about blocking a punch or kick, the student simply performed the movement associated with the key word being commanded. He proceeded to block every punch and kick effectively without any conscious thought. While this whole process may seem like Hollywood fiction, it is actually a perfect illustration of how the brain learns most effectively and efficiently. This is the key point we must take away from this example. Through research and data gathered while working with stroke victims, we now know it takes the brain approximately 3000 to 5000 repetitions in order for the victims to master new motor movement patterns. This is not something that ANYONE can short cut and still expect to master a task. Three to five thousand is the average range of repetitions it takes anyone to MASTER a new movement and put it into "auto pilot" mode. That doesn't mean the student can't feel it, repeat it and understand it intellectually after just a few reps, but they will not be able to come back the following week and perform the task without having to give it conscious thought. This is, in fact, one of the ways we test our students to ensure they are ready to stack the next learning block. We ask them to perform the movement they are working on while telling us what they had for breakfast. If they can perform the movement flawlessly without skipping a beat in the conversation, we know the brain has built a strong enough neural pathway that the student can be challenged with the next movement.

Three to five thousand reps sounds very daunting for most at first, but it is simply a fact of medical science and there is no way around it. However, the student should take heart in the fact that it only takes around 100 repetitions for the brain to actually create a new neural pathway. The century mark should be the goal in your lessons. If you can have your student perform 100 correct repetitions of the movement in a one hour lesson, you have firmly planted the seed for change and helped your student to truly make a lasting change in their golf swing. One hundred reps in an hour is a LOT of repetition, and you will have to be diligent to get it in. As you can imagine, there's not a lot of time for hitting many balls in a truly productive lesson, but ask your student whether they genuinely want to build a better golf swing or whether they want to keep hitting balls the way they are now, struggling from one day to the next. Once the pathway is built with that foundation of 100 reps, the brain will begin to "insulate" those neurons in the pathway with a fatty substance called myelin with continued repetition. This myelination acts as insulation that allows the neurons to fire faster and is a critical biological response to learning. The thicker this pathway becomes by being wrapped in more and more myelin, the more automatic the task becomes for the student. However, this process is a rather slow one and varies from one person to the next. The process of "myelinization" takes anywhere from a few days to a couple of weeks, providing further proof that giving a student a swing "tip" is a useless piece of advice over the long term. Learning the golf swing is a neurological process that requires physiological change in the brain and because of the biological processes involved, REQUIRES TIME! To further help you and your students understand the learning process, I highly recommend reading *"The Talent Code"* by Daniel Coyle. It is a great book that details the learning process and will serve as an invaluable reference to understanding how to truly help your students improve.

Our hierarchy of learning for the golf swing has been set up in the particular sequence you saw earlier for a purpose and the drills and learning program are built around how the brain learns as you have just read. The first building block of the hierarchy is perfecting the setup. Once the setup has been mastered, the next step is stacking the weight transfer. If at any time there is a breakdown in one of the fundamentals of the setup, we must remove any instruction about the weight transfer and readdress the setup. This follows the process of neuromuscular re-education. This process should be continued throughout the course of building the student's golf swing. We may find ourselves addressing the downswing when there begins to be a breakdown in the takeaway. When this occurs, we remove each of the subsequent pieces and go back to readdress the proper movements necessary to perform the proper takeaway. This is due to the fact that so much of what occurs in the golf swing is cause and effect based. While this process may not necessarily be viewed as desirable by the student, it is necessary to impart real change in motor patterns rather than allow the student to expect to make any lasting change in his or her golf swing with a "quick fix." There are no quick fixes in the golf swing, only temporary ones.

It is imperative that you, as the instructor, not only clearly understand the way the brain learns but also clearly convey the process to the student. When the student fully comprehends that there is only one path to true, lasting change and improvement, they will have no choice but to embark on the journey with you and be more committed to the process. More importantly, understanding the underlying biological processes involved in learning will help them understand why they failed to improve in the past and give them further hope that they can improve going forward by following your guidance.

Review questions:

1. How many repetitions does it take for a person to master a new motor movement and why?

2. What is myelin and what role does it play in the learning process?

3. How many repetitions does it take for a new neural pathway to be created?

4. List the seven steps to the Rotary Swing Hierarchy of Learning.

Chapter 3: Push vs. Pull

The concept of "Push vs. Pull" is central to the Rotary Swing Tour. Sir Isaac Newton determined that all movement is either a push or a pull. You can envision this very simply by thinking back to the days where golfers actually walked the course with the assistance of pull carts. If you ever used one of these, you noticed right away that it was much easier to keep the pull cart moving in a straight line when you let it trail behind you and you pulled it. When you tried to push it from behind, you would invariably develop a little "zig-zag" path as the movement seemed less stable. But why?

When we look at the definition of a pulling motion in its simplest form, it is the act of moving something towards you; or towards center. A push is the exact opposite. If you are trying to push a box across the floor of your living room, are you effectively moving it away from you or toward you? The reason that the pull cart travels in a much straighter line when pulled is that the force acting upon it is always moving it toward a centralized point – YOU! When you stand behind it and push it, it could move in any number of directions, a full 360 degrees away from center. When we apply these concepts to the golf swing, some very interesting things begin to appear that make a lot of the old instruction adages like "get your left shoulder under your chin" obsolete. We would, in fact, tell the student to pull his right shoulder behind his head.

First off, let's define one of our goals in the golf swing that is a fundamental of the RST. That is the goal to create centered rotation around the spine. The spine serves as a perfect axis around which to rotate in the golf swing if you want to stay centered and not shift laterally off the ball. If that is our goal, then the next logical step is to look at the motion that would allow us to accomplish creating centered rotation.

In our pull cart example, we were only talking about pushing and pulling as it pertains to linear motion; ie. You walking down the fairway toward your next shot pulling the pull cart behind you. But the golf swing by nature is rotational, so we need to introduce two more concepts from Mr. Newton – centripetal and centrifugal force. By definition, centripetal force is: *the force that is necessary to keep an object moving in a curved path and that is directed inward toward the center of rotation (Webster's Dictionary).* The definition for centrifugal force is: *the apparent force that is felt by an object moving in a curved path that acts outwardly away from the center of rotation (Webster's Dictionary).* Technically speaking, centrifugal force is a "false force" that is simply a result of centripetal force. The reality is centrifugal force doesn't exist at all, and no object would continue rotating around a centralized point without the aid of centripetal force or gravitational pull. Rather, it would continue on in a straight line. However, centripetal force is very real, very powerful and amazingly efficient.

To fully understand centripetal force, imagine a ball on the end of a string attached to a stick. By moving the stick in a very small circular motion, the ball on the end of the string can be accelerated to terrific speeds with minimal effort by you. Your tiny hand movements are creating centripetal force and are always pulling in the opposite direction of the ball to keep it moving at the highest velocities. The bigger you make your hand movements, the slower the ball begins to move and the more effort you have to put into moving the stick to continue accelerating the ball. As part of these bigger movements, it also begins to become much more difficult to keep the ball orbiting on a constant plane. Upon reaching maximum speed, the string will naturally extend to 90 degrees in relation to the stick and the ball will travel on a single plane around the stick as long as the stick remains centered and moving with the same simple, tight little movements. The looser the movements, the more difficult it becomes to keep the ball "on plane."

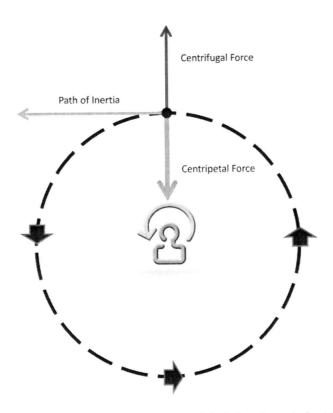

Figure 2 - A simple illustration of the concept of the ball on the end of a string.

It's not hard to see how this analogy directly relates to the golf swing as the concepts of plane and rotation are thrown about all the time in the instruction world. The key in the Rotary Swing Tour is that the plane is very easy to control when we understand how to create centered rotation when using the concepts of push/pull and centripetal and centrifugal force.

Let's first take pushing and pulling into a real world example as it applies to the golf swing. To do this, you'll need a partner. Stand upright and hold a club horizontally tight across your chest. From behind, have someone move you by pushing you from both sides of the club. You will notice if you look in a mirror, that your head will move about in both directions and you will likely not make a 90 degree turn. Now, have your partner pull the end

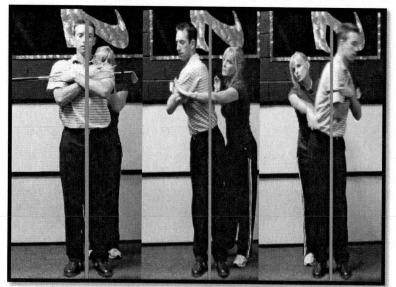

Figure 3 - Note how the head does not want to remain centered when pushed.

of the club back behind you. You will be amazed at how easily you can make a full shoulder turn and how much "tighter" and smaller the movements feel when compared to pushing. Take a look at the images to see this more clearly.

In the first image, when pushed from either side the head moves away from center, as does the rest of the body. For most golfers, this is exactly how they try and take the club back during the backswing. They simply push the left arm across the body by pushing from the left side and then wonder why they can't make a full shoulder turn. If you want to turn your back to the target, then, quite simply, turn your back. Let's look at what it looks when you are pulled from behind instead.

When being pulled, your head stays centered and the body can easily make a full shoulder turn without moving off the ball. You'll notice in the pull images that the head remains very centered. More importantly, you can feel this when your partner pulls you. This is the key to golfers of all flexibilities making a full shoulder turn and is the key to creating centered rotation around the spine. To date, I've yet to have a single golfer I've ever taught not be able to make a full 90 degree turn, no matter their age, fitness level or flexibility so the next time your student tells you he's not flexible enough to make a full shoulder turn, pull out this simple drill and watch his eyes light up.

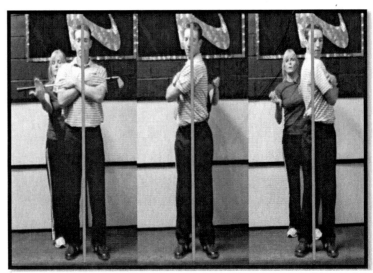

Figure 4 - This is what efficient rotation looks like when created by a pulling motion.

Once we've figured out why we want to pull and the benefits of doing so, the final goal is to look at exactly HOW we create this rotation. This is where a basic understanding of anatomy comes in handy for the instructor. Obviously, when doing the push/pull exercise earlier, you had someone creating the force for you by pulling or pushing on the golf shaft. Now, your muscles need to create that same force, but which ones? Fortunately, for creating rotation of the torso, there are relatively few muscles that you or your students need to be aware of. The first set of muscles that facilitate rotating the torso are the obliques. If you have your student sit at the edge of a chair and begin turning his torso from side to side with some speed, he will quickly become aware of his obliques. We'll talk more in detail about these muscles later. The second set of muscles the golfer will become aware of are a group of muscles in the back. Specifically, we refer to the lower trapezius and latissimus muscles. The lower trapezius muscle and rhomboid work to pull the scapula toward the spine (center) during the backswing and when done correctly, the golfer will feel the latissimus muscle activate. We generally don't refer to the rhomboid because most golfers haven't a clue what it is, nor can they feel it. Which is the exact reason we refer to the lat quite frequently. While it is the lower trapezius, not the latissimus, that is moving the scapula, most golfers can't feel it, but they can feel the lat. We'll discuss this more in depth later as well.

Using the scapular motion of gliding it across the ribcage in toward center helps create centered rotation exactly like what we are looking for and gets the golfer connected to the big muscles of his core. It's a win-win for the backswing. This movement is a key component for the golfer learning to create a "pulling" motion, which, as we have learned, is necessary for creating an efficient, centered rotation and will be a key to helping all your students create a 90 degree or greater shoulder turn in the backswing. While we have gone to great lengths in this chapter to emphasize the pulling motion desired to create centered rotation, it should be noted that this is not the only force that is going on. In fact, technically speaking, it is a "push-pull" throughout the golf swing. As an example, we emphasize pulling with the left oblique on the downswing because this is what helps clear the hips back out of the way, providing room for the arms on the downswing.   Most golfers push from the right side during the downswing and end up coming out of their spine angle. This is more instinctual for most but creates a number of common swing faults. When the golfer begins to focus his efforts on pulling, it is often a new feeling for him, so that's all he "feels." However, while he may feel the left oblique firing, the right oblique is also helping as they work in pairs in rotating the torso. It is important for the student to feel pulling over anything else in most cases, but as an expert golf instructor, you need to understand that both sides are working.

Review questions:

1. According to Newton, all movement is a push or a pull. In what direction does a push move and which direction does a pull move?

2. If the golfer wishes to remain centered, should he or she push or pull during the swing?

3. Explain centripetal and centrifugal force as it relates to the golf swing.

Chapter 4: In the Box

One of the primary keys to power in the golf swing is in the application of the large core muscles. The term, "in the box" is a central concept around which the Rotary Swing Tour model is based and refers to these large muscles in the torso. In this chapter, you will want to come to fully understand the term "in the box" and its opposite, "in the rectangle," as these are the simple terms we use to convey connection to the large and highly interconnected core muscles. Before we can come to an understanding of exactly what these terms mean, we must first review some basic anatomy. It is

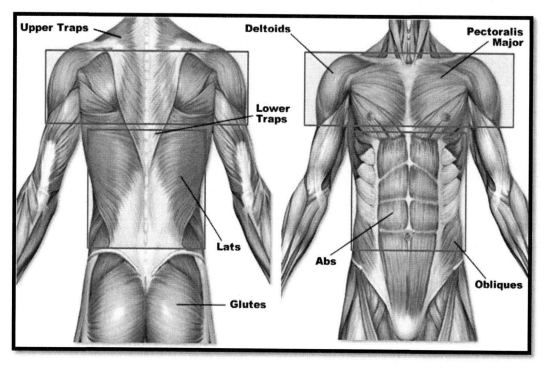

Figure 5 - These are the primary muscles you should fully understand their functions during the golf swing.

necessary to clearly define several of the major muscles of the body and their functions for the golf instructor to successfully teach a student how to move and where to move from in the golf swing. The goal is for the Rotary Swing Instructor (RSI) to fully understand how using the muscles in the rectangle is detrimental to achieving the goal of an efficient, repeatable golf swing. Conversely, the RSI needs to have a firm grasp of why staying in the box is essential for power and control.

The rectangle can basically be defined as the muscles of the neck and upper torso such as the trapezius and the muscles in the shoulders located both anteriorly and posteriorly. More specifically, it includes the following muscles and their corresponding functions:

- **Deltoids (Delts):** raises arm away from body to front, side, and rear
- **Upper Pectoralis Major (Pecs):** draws arm toward body and rotates upper arm inward
- **Trapezius (upper fibers) (Traps):** elevate the scapula causing a shrugging motion of the shoulders

The box can be defined as the muscles of the core of the body, both anteriorly and posteriorly. It includes the following muscles:

Rectus Abdominis (Abs): flexes spine and draws pelvis forward

Internal Oblique Abdominal (Obliques): flexes and rotates the trunk

External Oblique Abdominal (Obliques): flexes and rotates the trunk

Trapezius (middle fibers) (Traps): retract the scapula, drawing it towards the body's midline

Trapezius (lower fibers) (Traps): depress the scapula, drawing it inferiorly

Latissimus Dorsi (Lats): largest surface area of any muscle in the body; rotates and lowers arm, pulls shoulder blade back

Because it takes approximately 32 pounds of muscle to swing the golf club at 100 mph (*"The Physics of Golf"*, *Ted Jorgensen*), it is vital that we tap into the larger muscles of the core. The musculature of the upper back, neck, and arms is simply not large enough in most golfers to generate the necessary horsepower, nor is it designed to create rotation around the spine. Golfers who "swing from the rectangle" often appear to be making a steep chopping motion at the ball rather than an efficient rotary motion. This chopping motion is very inefficient, both from a swing mechanics and biomechanics perspective. When we engage the muscles in the rectangle, we anatomically lose our link to the large muscles "in the box." As you'll learn, the scapula is the central component to maintaining the connection to the large muscle groups. It is imperative that the proper position of the scapula be maintained during the swing for the golfer to remain in the box to generate power from the large core muscles. The following is from the Journal of the American Academy of Orthopedic Surgeons:

> *"This scapula is pivotal in transferring forces and high energy from the legs, back, and trunk to the delivery point, the arm and hand, thereby allowing more force to be generated in activities such as throwing than can be done by the arm musculature alone. This scapula, serving as a link, also*

stabilizes the arm to more effectively absorb loads that may be generated through the long lever of the extended or elevated arm."
W. Ben Kibler, MD and John McMullen, ATC
Journal of the America Academy of Orthopedic Surgeons, Vol 11, No 2, March/ April 2003

In short, allowing our shoulders to shrug, thereby getting into the rectangle, typically results in a weak, armsy slap at the golf ball as the golfer anatomically loses the link to the large muscles of the back. It is imperative for the student to learn how to get into the box and remain there for the duration of the swing into impact.

Figure 6 - What muscles do you feel engage when shrugging your shoulders up vs. having them depressed?

Students can get the feeling of getting into the box by depressing their shoulders and retracting them slightly. This brings us to our first set of cue words, "Shrug/Depress." When students shrug their shoulders, they should immediately feel all the muscles in their upper shoulders and neck area engage. If they pull their shoulders forward and up, they may notice the pectoralis major engage as well. When students depress their shoulders and retract them slightly, they will feel their Latissimus (lats) muscles engage -- think good posture or "military" posture. When they feel these muscles engage, they are, effectively, in the box. The shoulders and chest should be relaxed and feel very "open". The abdominals should now be engaged by the student to add stability and remove any excess lordosis (forward curvature; swayback) in the spine. Have them pull their belly button in toward their spine to properly support the lower back. They have now established a connection to the larger muscles in the core of the body. If, at any given time during the course of the swing, the shoulders are allowed to shrug and get out of the box and into the rectangle, the link to the core is broken, and it is difficult to regain during the downswing. If the student doesn't reconnect at some point, he is now forced to swing the golf club with the shoulder and arm musculature alone, with minimal assistance from the larger core muscles.

Few golfers can reconnect during the transition or downswing, and it is simply an inefficient and extra move to do so. Lorena Ochoa is a good example of a golfer who disconnects going back but then reconnects coming back through. Jim Furyk is another example. You can easily see the inefficiencies in these two golfers' swings and imagine how difficult it would be to teach the typical amateur these moves. Therefore, it is paramount that the student remains in the box throughout the swing, to build the simplest and most powerful swing possible.

Review questions:

1. Define the terms "Box" and "Rectangle."

2. Why is it important for the golfer to remain "In the Box" during the swing.

3. Are there muscles in the "Rectangle" designed to create rotation around the spine?

4. What are the primary muscles in the "Box" that create rotation?

Chapter 5: The Grip

The grip is another fundamental of the golf swing that has been taught numerous different ways over the years. From Hogan's weak grip to Ernie's strong grip, each has had his preference. When we look at the grip from an outside perspective, there are two requirements that we must first consider. The first is neutral joint alignment, and the second is what factors allow the clubface to be squared at impact most efficiently while still allowing a free release of the club.

Figure 7 - Note the "rounded" appearance of the shoulders when the palms face the front of the thighs.

When referring to NJA, the most common myth regarding the grip is that you should grip the club based on how your hands naturally hang at address. For instance, when you take your setup position without a club, if your arms naturally face the front of your thighs at address, you should grip the club with a stronger grip, and if they face the sides of your thighs, you should have a more neutral grip. Of course, this is ridiculous advice; not to mention potentially harmful causing undue stress to the shoulders and right elbow. No one's arms naturally hang and face the front of their thighs, this is simply a by-product of bad posture. This happens when the golfer allows the shoulder blades to protract, which creates a slumped or rounded appearance of the thoracic spine (the mid to upper back area). From this position, the golfer must rotate his arm 90 degrees or more to grip the club; not to mention the issues it creates with the swing itself. With the shoulder blades retracted and in neutral, the palms naturally face each other and make it very easy to take a grip that meets the requirements mentioned earlier.

In this neutral position, the "Vs" in the thumbs point vertically,

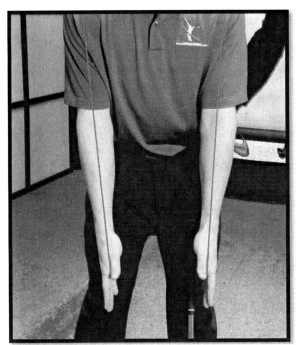

straight back up the arms. Yet, as the left arm reaches slightly across the body to grip the club, a slight clockwise rotation of the arm occurs and the shoulder blade protracts slightly. The larger chested the person, or the bigger arms they have, the more this protraction and rotation will have to occur to grip the club without bending the left arm. This

Figure 8 - Note the direction of the "Vs" when the arms are in NJA.

movement turns the "V" to a slightly stronger position where it is pointing to the right side of the head. As you move to position the hand with the pad of the palm over the handle, which is necessary for increased leverage, this further moves the left hand into a stronger position. As the last three fingers of the left hand cinch up to secure the club and the thumb and forefinger are pinched together, the shape of the "V" will fully take place and the final grip will be in a slightly stronger than neutral position. This allows the clubface to

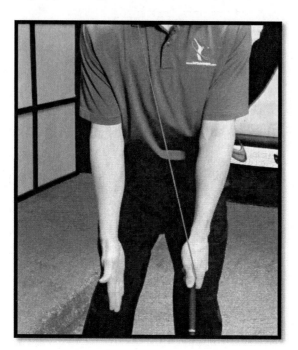

square more easily with minimal manipulation of the hands through the hitting area, all while protecting the joints from undue stress.

The right hand also has to work across to the center of the body where the club will be at address, but does so a little differently. In order to avoid significant scapular protraction created by reaching across the body to take the grip, the golfer employs "axis tilt" by bumping the hips slightly toward the target while keeping the head stationary. This tilts the spine away from the target while moving the right arm closer to the club so that it can take its position. While there is some protraction of the scapula, it should be minimized. The right arm will work across the body maintaining NJA with minimal rotation in a more "under handed" motion, placing the right hand in a position where the "V" points to almost directly up the right arm toward the right shoulder, which would be parallel to the "V" on the left hand. Because they are parallel, they cannot both point to the same spot, the "V" on the left hand will point to a spot slightly closer to the head of the golfer while the "V" on the right will point to a spot further from the head, toward the shoulder. This puts both hands in a balanced position that is neutral so they can work together to square the club.

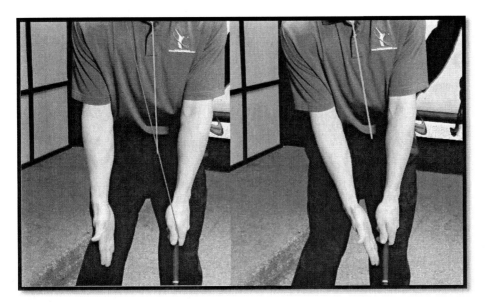

Figure 9 - Note the green line leans away from the target as the right hand is brought to the club correctly rather than protracting the shoulder blade and reaching across the body.

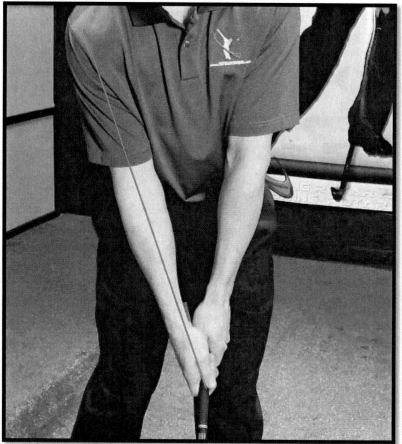

Figure 10 - As the right hand is brought onto the club, the wrist remains in neutral, causing the "V" to point directly back up the right arm toward the right shoulder.

Grip Pressure

We are very fortunate to work with Dr. Jeff Broker, who is on the Rotary Swing Advisory Board and is a leading researcher in the field of grip pressure. His research of golfers primarily at the lower handicap level has revealed one thing conclusively and that is that grip pressure is NOT constant throughout the swing. Unequivocally, grip pressure changes throughout the swing, starting from very light to significantly higher at impact.

Starting with a baseline for each golfer's maximum grip pressure (MGP) being benchmarked at 100%, the average pressure at address is in the range of 20% MGP. At the top of the swing during the change of club head direction, the grip pressure increases and then peaks to around 80% MGP at impact. In other words, good golfers are holding on nearly as hard as they can through impact. This should seem obvious due to the fact that the club effectively weighs as much as 100 pounds due to centrifugal force. However, the golfers do not realize they are gripping the club this tightly through impact. They feel as if it is constant, and that's a good feeling for the golfer to focus on because tension at the wrong times will inhibit the proper movements and decrease speed. Just like all things in the golf swing, the proper timing makes all the difference.

That being said, there are a couple of key points that need to be made regarding pressure points in the grip. The first has to do with the last three fingers of the left hand. Because of where the muscles that move them attach in the left forearm and both the pulling action of the left arm in the downswing and the uncocking (ulnar deviation) of the left wrist in the downswing, it is imperative that these three fingers securely grasp the club. The left hand's primary job coming into impact is to control both clubface direction and loft while uncocking the left wrist. The uncocking places the left wrist in a secure position, limiting unnecessary unhinging. This is particularly important to learn early on for beginning golfers as the most common swing fault at impact is this unhinging of the left hand, commonly referred to as flipping or cupping. With the left wrist fully uncocked, flipping the club becomes very difficult, and the stability provided by this motion will help significantly with clubface control.

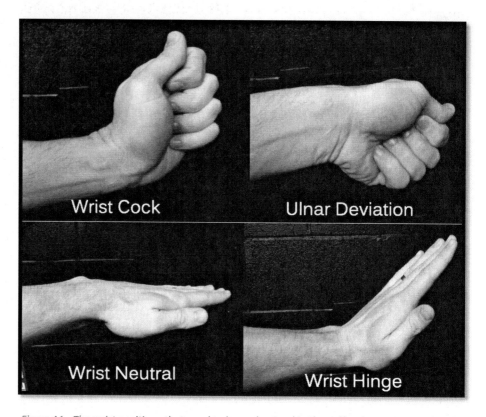

Figure 11 - The wrist positions that need to be understood in the golf swing.

While the right hand assists with controlling loft and, to a lesser degree, clubface angle, its role is no less important. The right hand is primarily responsible for transmitting speed from the trunk to the club head and, obviously, it can only do so through its contact points on the club, making them of supreme importance. There are three primary pressure points on the right hand that the golfer must become aware of to accelerate through and control impact. They are the proximal phalanx (the bone at the base of the finger) of the index

and middle two fingers. These key points will be responsible for transmitting forces created by the rotation of the trunk, the right pec and the extension of the right tricep, to name just a few. If the golfer is not aware of these points and doesn't learn to monitor them, he can struggle with both a lack of clubhead speed and a lack of clubhead control. They are also vital for having a sense of control of the golf club during the backswing and will be one of the key focus points in the Right Arm drills used later in this book.

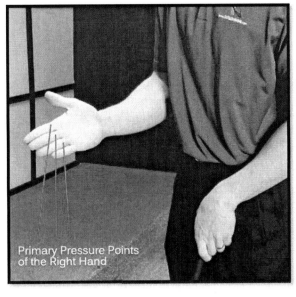

Primary Pressure Points of the Right Hand

Figure 12 - These three points are crucial for directing force in the downswing and sensing the clubface and lag.

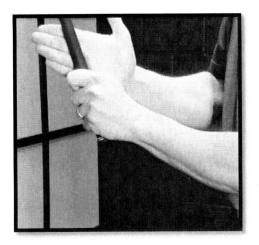

To provide a little more feel, dexterity and sensitivity for the index finger, there is often a gap between it and the middle

Figure 13 - Note how the club runs through the fingers on the right hand. For speed in the downswing, it is critical that the club not rest high in the palm. Think of the way the club sits in the right hand similar to how a fishing rod would rest in the hand while making a long cast.

finger. This positions the club slightly more toward the knuckle, or proximal interphalageal. In working with your students, you'll simply focus on the pad of flesh near the base of each finger.

Once these fingers are positioned correctly, the last necessary piece is to secure the thumb to the side of the palm where the "V's" are formed. This is imperative for the right hand. You will be able to detect golfers who are primarily just swinging with the left arm and not applying force from the right side simply by observing this position at address before they ever move the club. Golfers who don't use the right hand to transmit force will tend to have a space between the thumb and hand, making it more difficult to sense the club in the right index finger and requiring that they over use the left hand at the top of the swing to prevent the club from falling down in between the space between the thumb and right hand. Securing the thumb and hand together allows the right hand to properly support the club at the top of the swing while helping secure the right index finger in place on the grip.

Review Questions

1. Should the thumb and side of the hand have a space between them or be pinched together?

2. Where should the "Vs" of each hand point?

3. Describe the key pressure points in each hand.

Chapter 6: Setup

The setup is the one fundamental in the golf swing which every golfer can execute correctly every time. The goal for our setup is to ensure that our bodies are anchored to the ground in such a way that will provide a stable, centered platform for the rotation of the upper torso and that the proper muscles are engaged for correct posture, stability, and power. Our goal for this chapter is to become educated in the proper means of getting our students set up correctly every time. We also need to be aware of the most common setup flaws and their impact on the rest of the golf swing.

Critical Thinking: List 4 common fundamentals of setup taught in the golf industry today

1. _____

2. _____

3. _____

4. _____

Let us first discuss proper setup position which should include all of the following elements:

- Stance width: 2 inches outside of neutral joint alignment
- Weight centered over the center of the ankle joints (or slightly forward of that)
- Spine in neutral joint alignment
- Shoulders blades feel retracted (in neutral)
- Lower abdominal muscles engaged to remove excessive curvature of lumbar spine
- Arms: hanging naturally under the shoulders and the hands under the chin
- Elbows: "Pits" facing directly forward toward the target line (left pit will be rotated slightly away from the target with a grip that is stronger than neutral)
- Ball position: directly off the left ear
- Axis Tilt: 2-10 degrees of tilt depending on build, shot and club

Figure 14 - From down the line, a view of the joints in neutral. Note that the red line marking the "tush line" is considerably behind the heels when viewed from this angle. This clearly indicates the weight is back over the ankles rather than being over the balls of the feet. From this position, it is easy for the golfer to feel the powerful glute muscles engage right from the setup for stability in the swing.

Stance width: 2 inches outside of neutral joint alignment

Before we can further discuss stance width, we must first understand the definition of Neutral Joint Alignment (NJA). This term refers to when the joints of the body are in neutral, such as when, from a lateral view perspective, a straight line can be drawn from the center of the ear hole down through the center of the shoulder and hip joints, the back of the knee joint and through the center of the ankle joint. In the image to the left, you can see NJA from the side in regards to the center of the ankle lining up with the back of the knee which lines up with the center of the hip, which in turn, lines up with the center of the shoulder.

In addition, when observing the anterior view, NJA when referring to the lower body can be defined by a straight line running directly through the center of the hip joint, the knee and the center of the ankle. We wish the student to set up with the center of each ankle approximately 2 inches outside of this neutral joint alignment position. This is not an arbitrary measurement. This is the widest the stance can be in order to prevent lateral head movement from occurring throughout the golf swing while still allowing for a proper weight transfer. In other words, this position will allow us to provide a wide, stable base without forcing the upper body to shift laterally to transfer weight. It is important to understand lateral head movement will dramatically affect the balance of the golfer and the ability to consistently strike the ball cleanly. If the head is forced to move laterally in the backswing, the natural bottom of the swing arc moves with it. An excessive lateral shift must now be employed in the downswing, which will create movement linearly towards the target. The resulting downswing will can lead to a loss of speed and make it harder to keep the bottom of the swing arc consistent. Some head movement is normal, but RST strives to minimize it in order to preserve the swing center. As discussed in an earlier chapter, stance width is determined by the width of your pelvis, which can be easily established by locating the boney "hip bones" that tend to protrude on the front and side of the lower abdomen. On average, these bones sit about "2 finger widths" outside the center of the hip socket. The width of two fingers is close enough to establish neutral joint alignment and achieve the proper stance width.

The image of the skeleton on the next page shows NJA of the hip, knee and ankle. Note that the red line runs directly through the center of these joints. From this position, the golfer should go approximately 2" wider on either side for the proper stance width.

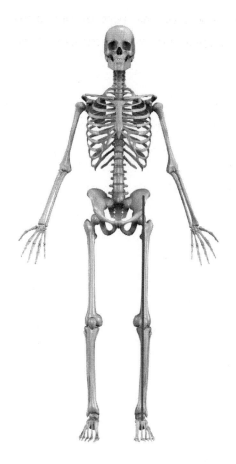

Figure 15 - When viewed from face on, a straight line drawn from the center of the hip socket will go straight through the center of the knee and the center of the ankle.

Weight centered over the center of the ankle joints

If we refer once again to the lateral view anatomical diagram provided earlier, we can plainly see the line runs from the back of the knee joint directly through the center of the ankle joint. This is the way our body was designed to bear weight in order to be balanced and support the weight of the rest of our body.   We want to accomplish much of the same when setting up to a golf ball.

Traditional instruction repeats to us over and over again that the weight should be on the balls of our feet. This is not the way the body is intended to bear its weight and remain balanced. In order to remain centered and balanced and fight the significant centrifugal forces occurring through impact, we must prepare ourselves to utilize our bodies' anatomical design. Having the weight centered over the ankles at address not only moves our weight back such that we can fight the inertia of the club during the downswing but also allows the two "chunkiest" muscles in the body to be fully engaged to provide stability for the rotating torso. The gluteus muscles will be engaged more effectively when the weight is back over the ankles, providing a tremendous amount of stability and power for the golf swing. As the golfer moves his weight toward the balls of the feet, the gluteus muscles begin to transfer the load to the quadriceps, or the front of the thighs. The primary role of these muscles is to move the lower leg away from the body (imagine kicking a soccer ball). They are not designed to support the hips for the rotation that is required during the downswing; however, the gluteus muscles serve this role perfectly. We establish the golfer in a truly balanced position with his weight on his ankles for this reason as well as the fact that it is necessary for rotation in the downswing, which we'll cover in more detail later.

Let us briefly discuss how we can get the student into this position with the weight centered over his ankle joints at address.   The procedure for the correct setup should be as follows:

- Stand straight, "in the box," and firm the knees

- hinge from the hip, keeping the spine neutral, which will cause the backside to protrude behind
- the student should feel the weight shift back into their heels to the point that their toes begin to raise up off of the ground
- once the weight is all the way back into the heels, relax the knee slightly and the student should feel the weight now centered over the ankle joints
- bump the left hip slightly toward the target while keeping the head stationary, creating axis tilt
- have the students roll the ankles in slightly

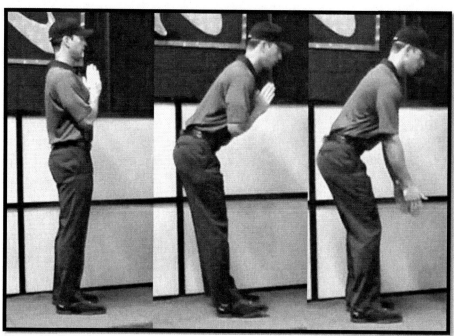

Figure 16 - Note the sequence. Good posture is established first, then the hips hinge, keeping the spine intact, then the knees are relaxed slightly.

Now that we have systematically discussed the "How" of the setup, let us take a moment and examine the "What" of each step in the process. We have the student stand straight and lock the knees because it is very easy to introduce excessive knee flex when first setting up to the golf ball. Excessive knee flex will shift the primary balancing joint away from the hip to the knees and the weight forward onto the balls of the feet, exactly what we are trying to prevent since the knees are not designed to rotate and that is required in the downswing. Once the weight gets into this position, as the student initiates the backswing, the weight is generally going to continue to move forward further onto the balls of the feet. This will cause one to engage the improper muscles in the lower body, namely the quads. With the weight forward and the quads engaged, as the student transitions into the downswing, the student will be putting unnecessary and potentially harmful stress on the knee joint and not be able to properly engage the hip muscles necessary for stability. The knee joint is a hinge joint. The function of a hinge joint is to allow forward and backward movement, mainly in one plane. This means that it is designed for extension and flexion only. With the weight on the balls of the feet, we have now placed the burden of rotational movement onto the knee joint since the primary balancing joint is no longer the hip, but the knee. This is a function it is not designed to perform. Thus, we can see that it is imperative to ensure health and safety that excessive knee flex not be introduced in the setup. If your students question this, simply have them place all their weight on their left over the ball of the foot and try rotating. Then, have them shift all their weight back over the ankle and rotate again. They will be able to easily feel how much strain is placed on the knee when on the balls of the feet.

Proper hinging from the hips ensures that we will not introduce any excessive curvature of the spine during setup and ensure the weight is moved away from the balls of the feet. When one hinges from the hips appropriately and the weight shifts back into the heels, combined with relaxing the knees slightly, the weight is centered over the ankle joints. We use the cue words "sway forward, sway back" to help students to find this position naturally on their own. Have your students stand straight up and close their eyes. Now, instruct them to sway forward allowing their weight to go to the balls of their feet and then sway back allowing their weight to go into their heels. When they've performed this motion several times, instruct them to stop when they feel balanced and relaxed, as if they could not be easily knocked off balance if pushed from any direction. The brain will inevitably have them feel most balanced in the anatomically correct position, centered over their ankle joints. In addition to the reasons discussed previously, when the weight remains balanced in this position, the student has ensured that the large muscles of the hips will bear the rotational forces of the swing, and the proper muscles can be used for power and stabilization.

The hip is a ball-and-socket joint in which the ball-shaped head of the femur fits into the cup-like cavity of the pelvis. Of all joint structures, a ball-and-socket joint gives the widest range of movement and is designed to allow for rotation. Given the rotational nature of the golf swing, it is imperative that the weight be centered over the ankle so that the hip can rotate during the swing. The final step in the setup, the slight rolling inward of the ankles, is performed to stabilize lateral hip movement. If the weight is on the outer portions of the foot, the hips have much more freedom to move laterally, an undesirable trait for the golf swing. Therefore, this move is performed in order to engage specific hip stabilizer muscles that quiet the lateral movement of the hips. Lastly, check that the weight distribution is approximately 50-50 between the right and left feet.

Spine: Neutral Joint Alignment

For health and safety issues, as well as increased rotational mobility, we want to ensure that the spine remains in NJA throughout the golf swing. We do not want any excessive curvature of either the upper or lower spine at setup. The spine consists of 33 ring-like bones called vertebrae, with 26 movable components within the spine. These components are linked by a series of mobile joints. Sandwiched between the bones in each joint is the intervertebral disc, a springy pad of tough, fibrous cartilage that compresses slightly under pressure to absorb shock and load. Strong ligaments and many sets of muscles around the spine stabilize the vertebrae and help control movement. The spine has five main regions, each with its own type of vertebrae: seven cervical vertebrae in the neck, 12 thoracic vertebrae in the mid and upper back, five lumbar vertebrae in the lower back, five sacral vertebrae in the sacrum and four fused coccygeal vertebrae. Our main concerns are the cervical, thoracic and lumbar regions.

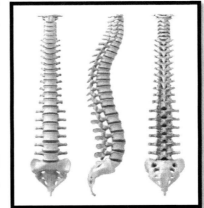

At setup, we must examine the cervical spine first. Most students will tend to look down at the golf ball at address, causing excessive forward bending, or flexion, of the cervical region. This must be eliminated by having the student stand upright until their cervical spine is in NJA.   Then bend only from the hips to maintain   NJA,   keeping   the   spine   intact.

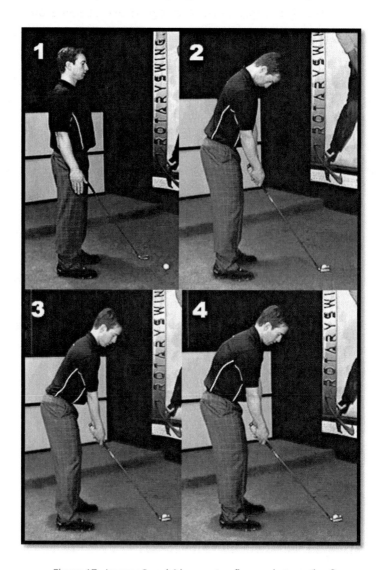

Figure 17 - Images 2 and 4 have setup flaws, what are they?

In Figure 17, the two images on the left demonstrate neutral posture while standing and in the golf setup. The top right picture shows bending primarily at the cervical spine whereas the bottom right picture demonstrates bending both in the thoracic spine and "at the waist." The bottom right picture shows one of the most common setup flaws that cause numerous swing issues and that is the excessive rounding of the thoracic spine. This setup severely limits rotational mobility. We must ensure that the student does not slump or round his shoulders at address, causing setup position. This is a typical result when golfers protract the shoulder blades in an effort to move the hands in front of the chest to grip the club and leads to the golfer being disconnected from the core muscles. Once a student is disengaged from his core, he will have little choice but for his force of movement from the top of the backswing to come from "the rectangle," rather than from the hips and lower body, without making a significant compensatory move. In addition, protracted shoulder blades allow the forearms to pronate, which will impair proper right arm flexion later in the backswing and require excessive rotation of the humerus during the backswing. To summarize, excessive curvature of the thoracic spine will most likely result in an inefficient, out-to-in swing path for the higher handicap player.

The final part to examine is the lumbar spine. In an effort to get their backs to NJA, students quite often impart excessive arching of the lower back, or lordosis. This is also a common trait in golfers because some instructors have advocated "sticking the rear out" at address. This sway back appearance can easily be eliminated by having the student engage their lower abdominal muscles. It is the responsibility of the instructor to ensure that the lumbar spine is not overly arched at address as this puts the student at greater risk for lower back injury. If your student complains that he feels tension or pain in his low back area after getting him into the proper setup, it is most likely that he simply needs to "pull his belly button in" toward his spine and that will remove the discomfort.

Arms: hanging naturally under the shoulders

The arm should remain tension free at setup. When this is performed correctly, the shoulder and elbow will be in NJA. The arms should hang naturally underneath the shoulders with the elbows directly beneath the shoulders. The hands will hang naturally underneath the chin, and the "elbow pits" will face away from the body. This is critical for numerous reasons but, at a minimum, understand that it is NJA.

Note that when viewed from face on, neutral posture has the "elbow pits" facing directly forward with the palms facing the thighs. When the golfer protracts the shoulder blades and gets into poor posture, the elbow pits face inward, and the palms now move in front of and face the front of the thighs. This position is extremely common and not only leads to common swing faults such as crossing the line at the top but can lead to injuries of the elbow and shoulder.

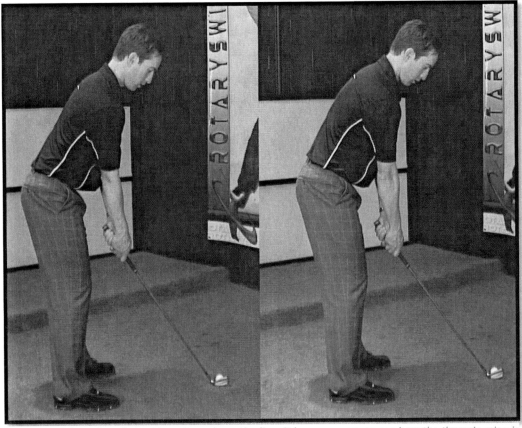

Figure 18 - When viewed at address from down the line, it becomes easy to see how the thoracic spine is rounded when the golfer rotates the elbows to point away from the body in the picture on the right. It is critical to keep the right elbow in neutral.

Ball Position

The ball for stock shots should be positioned directly opposite the left ear. When referencing ball position, instructors should not refer to the feet. The left ear or logo on the shirt is good, simple reference. This is by no means an arbitrary position; rather, it is based on the natural bottom of the swing arc. The bottom of the swing arc is where the club and left arm reach maximum extension during the swing, opposite the left shoulder. (Note that, in the case of golfers with significant axis tilt at impact, this can be considerably ahead of where the divot would bottom out. For the purposes of our discussion, we will be considering the bottom of the swing arc to be the deepest point of the divot.) We want the ball placed slightly behind that position in order to strike the ball with a descending and clean blow. This ball position should remain constant for every club in the bag on any stock shot. This is a common question we hear frequently. The simple answer is, do the width of your shoulders change on each shot? Of course, they don't, so the bottom of the divot should pretty much stay the same.

Instructors must be aware of the student getting the ball too far back in the stance, directly opposite the sternum, for example, as this is an extremely common fault. When the ball is too far back in one's stance, proper weight transfer cannot occur through impact without hitting a thin shot or missing the ball completely without some sort of compensation. Conversely, when the ball is placed too far forward in the stance, excessive lateral movement would have to be introduced in order to strike the ball cleanly and this tends to lead to a severely in to out swing path, especially for the better player. Neither of these scenarios is desirable, and both should be avoided. If the ball position is correct, the student's left ear will be slightly behind the back of the ball at setup when viewed face on.

Shrug/Depress

This is a simple exercise that we introduced earlier when discussing getting in the box. We discuss it more in detail here because it is a key drill that you will be having your students perform before taking their address position if they continue to exhibit bad posture at setup. Have the student should stand at attention facing the instructor. Ask the student to shrug his shoulders so they rise up towards his ears.

Now, ask the student to depress his shoulders, feeling as if he is pulling his shoulders down and reaching for the floor with his hands. Ask which muscles he feels engage when performing this motion. The correct answer should be the latissimus muscles. Be sure to walk around the back side of the student and hold the lat muscles to feel exactly where they should be engaged. As they hinge forward, you want to ensure they feel as if they remain in the box and they will notice some activation of the muscles in the middle of the back as they fight the forces of gravity pulling down on the arms. This is a healthy activation of the mid back muscles that is necessary to maintain our good posture that we had while standing erect.

A key component to this is ensuring that there is no excess tension, and the muscles are simply engaged, as we want to keep fluid athleticism in the golf swing, and excess tension will make this impossible. Use the example of a gymnast attempting to hold himself up on parallel bars. This example is quite effective at giving students a kinesthetic sense of what they're trying to accomplish. Emphasize to the student that the lat muscles must remain engaged in this manner throughout the golf swing and into impact because this is what will keep them "in the box" and allow maximum energy transfer from the big muscles to the club.

Review questions:

1. Define neutral joint alignment and its significance in establishing a proper setup.

2. What is the proper stance width, and what is its significance?

3. Where should the weight be balanced at address?

4. How does a golfer achieve proper spine alignment?

5. Where do the arms hang in posture?

6. How does proper ball position relate to setup and the bottom of the swing arc?

Chapter 7: Weight Shift

Rotary Swing Instructors must have a firm understanding of one of the key goals of the swing model, to utilize a proper right-to-left weight shift (for a right-handed player) just as we would in any other throwing or hitting sport. Most amateur golfers underestimate the importance of this simple yet critical step in the golf swing, specifically in getting back to the lead leg in the downswing. We could have the best takeaway in the world, but if we are attempting to hit the ball off the back foot, we are always going to struggle. It is also a matter of power. Research from Science and Motion in Germany has shown that a proper weight shift contributes 14.4% more club head speed when compared to an improper or no weight shift swing.

Let's take a moment and examine throwing mechanics. With respect to the mechanics of a baseball throw, Dr. Ross E. Vaughn of Boise State University states the following:

> *"Throwing is a fundamental skill that is often overlooked by coaches at all levels. Many coaches believe that throwing ability is: you have it, or you don't. Although some athletes have more natural ability than others, almost everyone can improve his or her throwing by understanding and practicing proper throwing mechanics. One doesn't have to be large or exceptionally strong to throw hard. A high velocity throw is largely the result of proper technique rather than brute strength. An accurate, hard throw involves a synchronized sequence of four motions: a stride, hip rotation, trunk rotation, and arm movement. The goal of this sequence of motions is to achieve maximal hand and ball velocity at the point of release. The throwing sequence begins with a step in the direction of the throw. As the stride foot hits the ground, the other foot braces against the ground to provide stability and leverage for the remaining movements of the throw. Hip rotation is the next element in the throwing sequence. Hip rotation simply refers to the natural tendency for the hips to open towards*

the thrower's target. It's important to remember that hip rotation must occur before trunk rotation. Unskilled throwers tend to rotate the hips and trunk at the same time. The longer you can keep your shoulders closed while your hips are opening up underneath them, the more power one is able to achieve in a throw. One thing to keep in mind when stepping towards the target is that it is critical that the hips rotate ahead of your shoulders. In conclusion, a high velocity throw is made possible by rapidly accelerating the arm and hand. The most rapid acceleration of the arm and hand occurs when the thrower's hips and trunk rotate in the proper sequence. Coaches should help athletes understand and practice the mechanics by ensuring that they do the following in sequence: stride in the direction of the throw and keep the stride short enough to allow maximum hip rotation; allow the arm to lag behind the hips and trunk so the athlete feels a slight stretch in the trunk and arm muscles; and extend the elbow at the same time that the upper arm is moving forward and turning inward."

Figure 19 - Note the sequence of both the weight shift and the unwinding of the torso and how they are similar to the golf swing.

The purpose of examining this example is to illustrate that weight shift is essential to most all sports that involve swinging or throwing and to point out many of the similarities between throwing a baseball and swinging a golf club. It is essential to teach our students the proper mechanics of weight shift if they wish to achieve maximum efficiency, speed and power in their golf swings. The correct kinesthetic sequence can be easily illustrated through a series of simple exercises.

Shift Right/Shift Left

In order to help the student obtain a basic kinesthetic sense of the weight transfer that occurs in the golf swing and how little movement is actually required, we can begin by doing a simple shift right/shift left drill. The student simply stands up straight facing the instructor and places his feet in the proper setup position, each foot 2 inches outside NJA. Now, have the student shift one inch to the right, placing the right hip just inside the right ankle. When done correctly he should feel as if he's pushing the right ankle into the ground. It is okay if the upper body moves a little bit while doing this; the purpose of the drill is to focus on transferring weight and how little the movement really is. Now, have him shift the hips three inches to the left. His left hip should be in NJA, and he should feel his weight pushing the left ankle into the ground. It is important to have the student do this multiple times, until he feels very comfortable and can feel himself driving the weight into the right ankle and then driving weight into the ground with the left ankle. The entire time he is performing this movement, begin ingraining the cue words Shift Right, Shift Left so the student's mind is trained to perform these movements automatically without having to think of what the terms mean.

Figure 20 - The purpose of this drill is to have the golfer become aware of the pressures he or she will feel in the feet when making a shift and to demonstrate how little movement is required to shift the weight.

Once he has become comfortable making this tiny shift going back to the right and then making the shift back to NJA on the left, have the golfer get in his setup and perform the same movements. Once in the address posture, he may struggle a bit more with this very simple movement, but it is an important continuation of the exercise because the student should now be able to feel the glutes activate. And this is what you want to emphasize during each shift. As the golfer makes the slight shift to the right, have him or her try and actively drive force into the ground by visualizing pushing the right ankle into the ground. As they go back to the left, you want them to push the left ankle into the ground. The glutes' primary role is stabilization in the golf swing, and it is imperative that the golfer become aware of these muscles by doing this simple isolation drill.

Of final note, it is crucial that the golfer not dominate the shift back to the left by pushing off the right side. This push will tend to move the golfer past NJA on the left and put them at risk for hip and back injury. The shift back to the left should feel as if it is almost exclusively done with the muscles in the left hip area and inner thigh (hip adductor group) for the student as most dominate with pushing off the right foot. As we move onto the next drill, learning to properly move from these muscles will bring the golfer into a perfect impact position; whereas, pushing from the right will open the hips up more than is necessary.

Shift Right/Shift Left/45* Hip Turn

This drill now asks the students to stack the Shift Right/Shift Left drill with a small hip turn that will simulate the downswing and impact positions. Once again, have the student take the address position with the feet two inches outside NJA. Have the student shift the right hip one inch to the right while planting the right ankle into the ground. Once the student can feel the right glute activate, have him "pull" himself back over to the left using only the muscles in the left hip area. The right foot should remain passive and low to the ground, the heel only moving inward toward the left foot as it is pulled off the ground by the shift to the left and the upcoming rotation. The sequence is shifting the left hip three inches to the left, driving the left ankle into the ground and adding 45° of hip rotation to the left. The hip rotation is created by pulling the left hip around behind the golfer away from the target, NOT pushing the right hip around toward the target, which will tend to create early extension of the spine. Of equal importance is the fact that by pushing off the right leg, the hips can rotate a full 90 degrees open in relation to the target line by the time impact occurs. This movement prevents the kinetic chain from "snapping" as the hips must decelerate during the downswing after their initial acceleration in order for that energy to be efficiently transferred out to the arms and club. Pulling from the left side ensures that hips will only move to about 45 degrees open to the target line by impact and will then slow down, as that is as far as these muscles can rotate the hip without help from the right side. The other benefit to pulling from the left side is that this will move the left hip into NJA, as that is how our muscles are designed to work. Without a pushing motion from the right leg, the left hip will stop moving toward the target once the left hip is centered over the left ankle. This "built-in stop" is a safety mechanism that keeps us from hyper-extending our joints and creating injury. We kill at least three birds with one stone with this one simple movement. This will require some deeply focused practice on your student's behalf to both feel these muscles and implement this movement into their golf swings. It will be virtually impossible to perform the correct movements at full speed at first while hitting balls. The student will immediately want to revert back to his normal tendencies, so it is vital to start out only hitting short shots at first and build up to hitting longer shots as the student begins to master the movement.

Have the student repeat the entire movement performing it to the right and back to the left and then doing it at speed until it becomes more natural. This exercise represents the entire active lower torso movement from setup to backswing and on through to impact. We say active because the hips do turn 45 degrees during the backswing, but that is not an active turn. You will learn that this is a result of the upper torso turn. This move must be mastered by the student before moving on to the takeaway.

Review questions:

1. List two examples of other athletic activities that utilize a right-to-left weight shift.

2. Explain the Shift Right/Shift Left drill and its significance.

3. Name two primary goals of the Shift Right/Shift Left/45° Hip Turn drill.

Chapter 8: The Takeaway

The takeaway move, which we refer to as Move 1, has been somewhat of an elusive mystery over the years in golf instruction. There have been many theories about how to position the club on plane, none of which have specified HOW to move the body to get

Figure 21 - During the takeaway, the shoulders will turn a full 45 degrees, and the arms and hands will have hardly moved from their address position.

there; and more specifically, which muscles to engage to do it. This chapter will examine exactly how the body is anatomically designed to move to efficiently accomplish the takeaway with minimal movement.

During the takeaway, approximately 80% of our weight will be transferred onto our right ankle, and this can be reinforced by the feeling of pushing the right ankle into the ground and the activation of the right gluteus muscle. This is the first distinguishing move of Move 1. As the club is started to be taken away, we must allow the right hip to shift to the right approximately 1 inch and the majority of the weight to transfer to the right ankle. Actively engaging the right glute is necessary for stability and power and also for the shape of the swing.

During the weight transfer, the club is also moving, but what is it that takes the club back? To answer this question appropriately, we must go back and examine the push versus pull discussion. A pull is an action that moves an object towards center; a push is a force moving an object away from center. In terms of rotation, these two forces are referred to as centripetal and centrifugal force, respectively. Given our understanding of these forces of motion, it should become quite clear to the instructor that we must invoke a pulling motion in order to turn the upper torso in a fashion that keeps us centered with minimal lateral movement of the head. This pulling motion can only come from the trailing hand side of our bodies during the backswing. In short, a pulling of the right shoulder blade in toward our spine on the backswing will move us towards center (our spine) and allow us to initiate rotation while remaining centered. This move also serves as a spine stabilizer during the backswing protecting the spine and, when done correctly, connecting us to the large muscles of the core. Let us now more closely examine how we move the right shoulder blade in the backswing.

In order to ensure that we are in the proper setup position, we must remember the discussion about being "in the box." To engage the box, have the students shrug and then depress their shoulders while standing upright and then take their setup. When they depress their shoulders, reference the example of a gymnast trying to support himself on the parallel bars. This will ensure that the students engage their latissimus muscles as they depress their shoulders. Be certain that they simply engage the lat muscles and do not exert any excessive force that creates tension in the back. Once they are in the box, they are now in position to perform the shoulder blade glide. In this movement, we are focusing on pulling the right shoulder blade slightly down and in toward the spine and engaging the right lat muscle.

Technically speaking, it is actually the lower trapezius and rhomboid that is responsible for moving the scapula in toward the spine and down into the box. However, most golfers lack the muscular awareness to feel these muscles engage. The latissimus, however, is the largest muscle, surface area wise, in the body and most golfers can feel this muscle engage during the takeaway if they stay in the box, which is why we focus on it. If the golfer were to perform the takeaway incorrectly and move into the rectangle during the swing, the lat will disengage which is the cue for the golfer and the instructor that the golfer is moving from the wrong part of the body and will now be disconnected from his powerful core during the swing. The instructor must train his eye and his hands to recognize when this disconnection occurs.

Figure 22 - This disconnected position on the right requires a complicated rerouting of the club to return back to the ball.

When the golfer gets disconnected during the takeaway, it leads to a disconnected position at the top where the right elbow flies away from the body, as can be seen in the picture on the right. From here, a much more complicated series of movements must occur in the downswing to get back to impact versus the image on the left where the right lat is still engaged and the right arm has remained in front of the body.

In the two images on the next page, you can see the area of the body and direction of movement to which we are referring. While it is a crude drawing for the sake of simplicity, it does illustrate three important pieces. First, it demonstrates where the shoulder blade naturally sits in neutral and demonstrates the direction it is being moved. Second, it illustrates the muscles the golfer should be feeling during this movement other than the lats. Last, it illustrates the direction that the actual muscle fibers of the lower trapezius run, showing why the shoulder blade is moving down and in, further into the box. This move is identical to the scapular motion a pitcher employs when throwing a baseball at high speed.

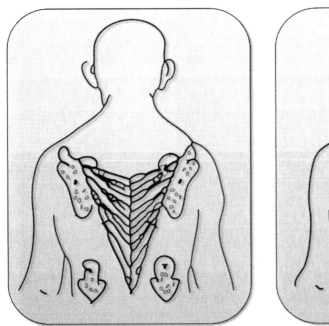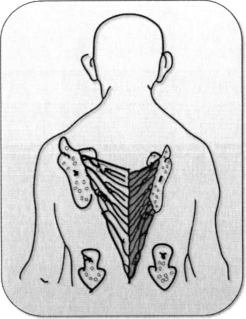

Figure 23 - During the takeaway, the right shoulder blade glides across the rib cage toward the spine and very slightly down.

This simple movement of the scapula down and in up to two inches will result in the shoulders moving 6-8 inches by the completion of the takeaway (club parallel to the ground), the hands moving 2 1/2 feet and the club moving approximately 2 1/2 yards. When performed correctly the upper torso has rotated 45°, and the hips have rotated minimally, as little as 0°. The reaction to the movement of the shoulder blade is the club being parallel to the target line with the club head in line with the hands. The hands should still remain centered in front of the chest, in line with the sternum. This will be a signal to the instructor that the arms have remained passive, a very important key to ensure that the club does not get taken too far inside when performing this move. Any form of arm swing around the body, especially from the lead arm, will cause the arms to work around the body and result in the club getting trapped inside and require excess use of the arms throughout the swing.

Before we discuss the role of the arms during the takeaway, we must also discuss the muscles that are primarily responsible for the rotation of the torso, the obliques. The obliques are the muscles that run down the side of your torso and attach to your hips to create rotation in the hips as well. While the shoulder blade glide initiates a centered turn, the obliques will carry the bulk of the load in continuing to rotate the torso. It is difficult for most golfers to feel the obliques in their swings, so we have a simple drill to help them. Have students sit in a chair with their arms across their chests and perform the shoulder blade glide while continuing to look forward. Have them pull their trailing shoulder as far behind them as they can and then repeat this on the other side. Have them begin to perform this action with some speed, and they will begin to become aware of the oblique muscles feeling stretched on one side while the other actively pulls the torso around.

Let us now turn our attention to the role of the arms during this move. As stated previously, the arms must primarily remain passive, meaning no excessive tension building up in the arms and no forceful movement with the arms and shoulders. In brief, the arms should remain straight with minimal right elbow flexion until midway

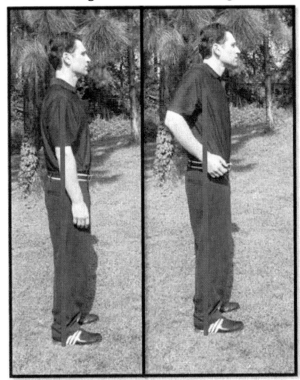

Figure 24 - As Al moves his elbow behind neutral (the red line), note how his shoulder elevates into this weak and disconnected position.

through Move 2. The right elbow bending early during the takeaway is a common error seen in most students due to pushing from the left side, forcing the hands behind the sternum. This move is detrimental for numerous reasons, but in terms of remaining connected to the core and "in the box," the instructor must understand that for every 2° the right elbow moves behind NJA (directly beneath the shoulder), the right scapula will elevate 1°, resulting in the student coming out of the box. This problem is being demonstrated by Rotary Swing Instructor Al Consoli in the images above. This forces the golfer into a position where, unless a compensatory move is made, he will be relying on the musculature of the arms, shoulder girdle and upper back to generate club head speed as opposed to using the larger muscles of the box.

Rotary Takeaway vs. Arms Takeaway

Let's examine the two images in Figure 25. In the image on the left, the golfer has clearly remained in the box, which is illustrated by the maintenance of the distance between his right shoulder and his right ear. He has successfully performed the right shoulder blade glide in addition to keeping his arms passive during the first portion of his backswing. His hands are directly in front of his sternum, and his arms have remained very straight. The club is in front of his body, and he is rotating from his core. The image on the right is based on the popular one plane swing model developed by Jim Hardy. The golfer has clearly come out of the box during the first portion of his takeaway, and in fact, the one plane model advocates it. A Rotary Swing Instructor should plainly be able to see that the golfer on the right has not turned his shoulders and has simply swung his arms across his chest with excessive right elbow flexion. As a result, notice the club is deep behind his "centerline" (the sternum when viewed face on) and is now in line with the far right side of his torso. Also, take note of the amount the right shoulder has shrugged at this point in his backswing. From the position the golfer has achieved, we now know it is anatomically impossible for him to fully utilize his core and efficiently transfer significant power from the large muscles in his trunk. Imagine trying to throw a knockout punch from this elevated shoulder blade position and you can feel the difference. While the club looks to be on plane, this is of very little significance. The golfer has no choice but to attempt to generate speed in his golf swing from simply using his arm and shoulder musculature with minimal assistance from the larger core muscles.

Figure 25 - In the image on the left, note how the logo on my shirt is clearly visible, a clear indication I have turned my torso.

Takeaway Drills

Communication is the key to being a good instructor. We must be able to not only demonstrate the movements to give the brain a clear picture of what it needs to do but also verbally communicate the appropriate means of performing a particular movement while associating those instructions with the proper feelings for the student. We must be able to provide the student with both an intellectual and kinesthetic awareness of how to perform each segment of the swing. The following drills will help the student be able to perform the proper takeaway movements by starting with simple drills and slowly introducing the arms and eventually, the club.

Rotation Drills - Arms Across the Chest

While standing upright, the student folds his arms across his chest, right hand on left shoulder, left hand on right shoulder. Ask the student to shrug and depress in order to feel himself get into the box while maintaining his posture. Now, have the student perform the right shoulder blade glide, pulling the right shoulder behind him to turn his shoulders 45°. Explain to the student that he should feel the shoulder blade glide across the rib cage, in toward the spine, and slightly down. Be certain that there is little to no hip rotation during this move. You should be aware that many students will begin to feel soreness in the mid back area while performing this drill. This is a definite indication that they are overdoing the glide movement. In truth, it is very subtle and should NOT reach its maximum range of motion during the takeaway. It is not just the shoulder blade that is moving the torso, but the obliques as well. The shoulder blade glide is simply initiating the movement while ensuring centered rotation and connection to the core.

The student should be able to perform this move relatively easily while remaining in the box. After performing this motion several times ask the student to stack both this move and pushing the right ankle into the ground. Hold the head steady if necessary, for we want to make sure that the head remains centered when doing this in the actual golf swing. Once the student can perform this standing upright, have him get in his posture, hinging from the hip, and repeat the drill. The feelings the student should be able to communicate to the instructor are the right lat engaging as the scapula is pulled towards center while remaining low on the cage and the right gluteus being engaged while the right ankle is pushed into the ground.

RSI Al Consoli demonstrating rotation created by pulling the right shoulder blade back toward his spine and slightly down to initiate the movement, while the obliques facilitate rotating the torso. Note that his head remains centered. If he were to try and "push" his left shoulder under his chin as the common instruction adage goes, the head would tend to move away from center as that's what a push does – moves objects away from the force of movement. In the case of the golf swing, a centered turn is easy to create when the focus is on pulling the right shoulder behind the head. The last thing to note is that his shoulders are rotating perpendicular to his spine, or 90 degrees to the ground while standing upright.

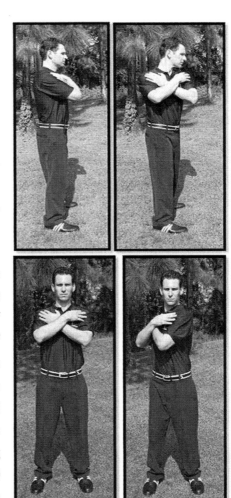

Figure 26 - This drill is very helpful to get the student focused on rotating the torso rather than what the arms are doing.

Once the student can perform the shoulder blade glide from an upright posture, have him setup and perform the same movements from his address position with his arms still across his chest.

Hands 1" Apart Rotation Drill

Of all the drills that can be used to teach a student the backswing, this is the one that you will find the most effective. Start out by instructing the student to get into his setup and allow his arms to hang naturally straight down, ensuring that they are straight. The palms should face each other, there should be approximately a one inch gap between the hands, and the fingertips should be even. Ask the student to perform the right shoulder blade glide and maintain this arm and hand position. The arms will be moved by the right shoulder blade glide and torso turn but should not move on their own apart from a slight amount of shoulder elevation (discussed in depth in the second half of the backswing, or Move 2). The right shoulder blade glide will provide 45° of torso rotation and 0° of hip rotation. When performed correctly:

- the fingertips will remain even
- the 1 inch gap will remain constant

- the hands will be directly in line with the sternum
- the right shoulder blade will remain depressed and in the box
- the hands will elevate slightly (discussed in Move 2)
- the right shoulder will still sit low and relaxed and not move up toward the right ear
- both arms should be completely straight.

If the student actively uses the arms, pushes from the left side, comes out-of-the-box or allows right arm flexion, the ideal position which was just described will be lost. The fingertips will be uneven, the right elbow bent, the 1 inch gap between the hands will be increased and the right hand will be on top of the left with a shrugged right shoulder. These are all clear signals to the instructor that the move is not being performed correctly. movement. In Figure 28, you can note several things. First, the upper torso has rotated fully 45+ degrees and the hands have remained

Figure 27 - Note that the hands have been moved by the rotating torso and have not moved independently to this point, other than some elevation.

centered in front of the sternum. Also, the right shoulder has remained depressed, creating the appearance of a lot of space between the right shoulder and the right ear. Last, there is clearly weight on the right ankle, and there has been a slight amount of shoulder elevation as the hands have begun to work slightly up in front of the chest from their address position rather than around.

Figure 28 - Al demonstrating the most common takeaway faults when performing the Hands 1" Apart Drill.

In Figure 28, you can see three common mistakes such as the right shoulder elevating up toward the right ear and early right elbow flexion. In the second photo, the left arm has clearly swung across the chest and effectively "pushed" the right hand deep behind the body. In the last photo, the turn and weight shift are good but there has been far too much shoulder elevation during this phase of the swing, leading to the club head working significantly to the outside and above the plane.

In summary, here is the sequence of Move 1:

- right shoulder blade glide; focus is on moving scapula in toward spine and slightly down
- torso turns 45°
- hips turn minimally, as little as 0°
- hips shift 1 inch right
- arms remain straight and directly in line with the sternum
- slight wrist set may be used to set the club into position
- obliques rotate torso.

Review questions:

1. How far should the head move during Move 1?

2. How much weight should be transferred into the right ankle during Move 1?

3. What takes the club back?

4. How far and in what direction does the scapula move during Move 1?

5. Explain the relationship between elbow flexion and its effects on the scapula.

6. What is the desired effect of using the keywords Shrug/Depress?

7. List five results of the Hands 1 Inch Apart drill.

8. How far do the shoulders and hips turn during Move 1?

9. List five characteristics of Move 1 when performed correctly.

Chapter 9: Completing the Backswing

Completing the backswing, or Move 2, is the movement from the time the club reaches parallel to the ground to the time the transition occurs, just before the club changes direction. Specifically, we are focusing on the shoulder turn and arm movements. To briefly summarize what occurs in this move:

- shoulders turn another 45° for a full 90° turn
- hips turn approximately 45°
- arms continue to elevate, hinging from the shoulders (Shoulder Elevation)
- the right arm hinges at the elbow (Right Elbow Flexion)
- rotation of the upper right arm (humerus bone) occurs

The important point that must be understood by the Rotary Swing instructor is that as the shoulders turn, the right shoulder blade glide is continuous during Move 2. It is this shoulder blade glide which is responsible for pulling the hips into the backswing. In Move 1 the right shoulder blade glide and obliques are responsible for turning the shoulders 45 degrees. In Move 2 the right shoulder blade glide and obliques pull the hips around to rotate 45 degrees. In other words, 45 degrees shoulder turn plus 45 degrees of hip turn gets the golfer's back to the target (i.e., 90 degrees of shoulder rotation). It is vital for the golfer to remain in the box for the duration of the backswing. It is quite common to see students begin to shrug their shoulders during this move. The focus should be on keeping the right lat muscle engaged for the duration of the backswing. If the student begins to shrug the shoulders toward the ears during the backswing, have the student stop at the top of the swing, "shrug" and then "depress" to create the connection in the mind for where the shoulder blade should sit at the top of the swing.

In the images below, note how close the right shoulder is to the head

Figure 29 - Note the space that is created between the right shoulder and the right ear when the golfer maintains the depressed scapula. Which looks more powerful to you?

in the image on the left. On the right, the right shoulder has much more space because the scapula is depressed.

For the most part, the arms have done very little at this point in the swing, and we usually emphasize this because almost all golfers do too much with their arms too early in their swings, which inhibits rotation and tends to get the arms deep behind the body. The arms do have a job to do during the backswing, and it is during Move 2 that we begin to focus on them.

The Rotary Swing model desires that the arms remain mostly passive throughout the backswing; whereas, most amateurs overuse the arms significantly. However, instructors must be aware of what we mean when we say "passive arms." This term implies that there is minimal conscious effort or movement of the arms swinging around the body or creating force in a way that overpowers the movement of the body. The arms should remain directly in front of the chest throughout most of the backswing until right elbow flexion pulls them across the body. To imply that the arms have no role other than to remain pinned to the torso is also inaccurate. This pinned arm position results in the club getting too far inside during Move 2. As a result, the swing plane becomes very flat. In order to prevent this from happening, the student must come to understand Shoulder Elevation and Right Elbow Flexion. These two movements are primarily responsible for the shape and plane of the backswing.

Shoulder Elevation

The term "Shoulder Elevation" is another one of our cue words. In medical terminology, the correct term would be "shoulder flexion", but elevation creates a better picture in the student's mind as to what is happening to the hands. In order to teach the student proper shoulder elevation, the following drill should be used:

Figure 30 - Shoulder flexion moves the hands from belt high to the bottom of the pectoral region in a vertical plane.

Ask the student to stand facing the instructor. Have him extend his arms straight in front of him at approximately belt high. While remaining in the box, have him elevate his hands to the base of his pectoral region. It is important that he keeps his shoulder blades depressed during this move in order to stay in the box and connected to his core. In brief, the hands elevate approximately three to six inches directly in front of the sternum. This is the extent of the shoulder elevation for the entire backswing. Take note of the photos above.

It is this Shoulder Elevation that keeps the club from getting too far inside during the backswing and is responsible for creating some vertical movement of the club to keep the club on plane and the hands in front of the chest. While we focus on shoulder elevation during Move 2, there is also a slight amount occurring during Move 1. As the instructor, you must watch for the club moving too low and around. If the club begins to work too far inside, you will want to introduce some shoulder elevation during Move 1 AFTER they have mastered the core movements of Move 1 discussed earlier.

Right Elbow Flexion

The term "Right Elbow Flexion" is another one of our cue words. The right elbow flexion is responsible for three main things in the backswing. First, it is the primary creator of vertical movement of the club during the backswing. Second, it helps get the club in a powerful "set" position at the top. Finally, it is the primary movement that pulls the hands across centerline. This right elbow flexion should not exceed 100° in most cases as doing so will require either the left arm to bend or the right arm to swing deep behind the chest. The flexion should occur late in the backswing, but before the back has reached the target and after the takeaway. Before the flexion takes place, the hands should still remain centered in front of the chest. To teach the student these critical movements, have them perform the following drill:

- Ask the student to stand upright, facing the instructor.
- Once again, have the student extend his arms straight in front of him at approximately belt high.

- The hands should be separated by a one inch gap.
- Now, ask him to perform the shoulder elevation, repeatedly moving the arms up and down in front of the chest.
- Once the hands reach the base of the pectoral region ask him to add 90° of right elbow flexion.
- Once the student can perform these simple tasks, ask him to grab his left thumb with the right hand and repeat the sequence: shoulder elevation, right elbow flexion. Ensure that the left arm remains straight during this movement.

Figure 31 - This sequence captures all the movements of the arms during the backswing.

Stacking Shoulder Elevation/Right Elbow Flexion with Rotation

Now, it is time for the instructor to integrate or "stack" the shoulder elevation and right elbow flexion elements of the swing with rotation.

- Ask the student to face the instructor.
- Once again have him extend his arms straight in front of him at approximately belt high.
- Have him grab his left thumb with his right hand.
- Have him perform shoulder elevation and right elbow flexion.
- While performing the right elbow flexion, make sure the student keeps the left arm straight and the right elbow flexion never exceeds 100°. *This may prove difficult for some students as they tend to collapse the left arm when performing the right arm flexion.*
- Now, have the student pull the right shoulder blade back to simulate the rotation in the backswing. The right arm should remain in front of the chest as the shoulders reach the top of the backswing.

Figure 32 - Performing the drill while in an upright posture.

The height of the hands at the top of the swing is primarily determined by the amount of shoulder elevation during the backswing and is a variable in the swing. In order to keep the arms in front of the chest, a golfer with longer arms will require more elevation than someone with a wider chest and shorter arms.

Putting It All Together

The next step in the stacking order is to integrate shoulder blade glide with shoulder elevation and right elbow flexion while having the student in his golf setup. This should first be done without a club.

Once the moves are mastered without a club, the club can slowly be introduced, then slowly work into hitting balls with the student.

- Have the student assume the proper setup.
- The student's arms should hang in neutral directly beneath the shoulders when viewed DTL and in front of his sternum viewed FO.
- Have him grab his left thumb with his right hand.
- Now ask him to perform the shoulder blade glide of Move 1.
- Once Move 1 is complete, add shoulder elevation and right arm flexion as he continues to pull his right shoulder blade behind him, rotating his torso.
- Ensure that the right upper bicep remains connected to the upper pectoral muscle and that the force of movement does not come from the left side.

Be certain that the arms do not begin to swing around the body but remain directly in front of the sternum, only moving in a vertical plane due to shoulder elevation. Again, be certain to use the cue words shoulder elevation and right elbow flexion. Most students will find this rather difficult to perform and want to "swing" the arms around the body. If at any time the instructor sees the student beginning to swing the arms across the body once we have added this hinge from the hips, immediately ask him to stand straight up and run through the sequence once again.

Figure 33 - From a bent over posture, the drill will be more challenging for the student, but the movements are the same.

It will be significantly easier for your students to learn the core backswing movements in this fashion, without a golf club. The moment the golf club gets introduced to the mix, there is much more momentum to deal with. The student will want to revert back to a movement that isn't focused on the proper muscular movements; rather, he'll be more concerned with what the club is doing. Doing the drills without a club allows the student to develop a new awareness for the muscles that are working without allowing the club to interfere. You will find that with ten minutes of work exclusively on this drill, your student will be able to make the movements without a club very well and have a fighting chance once the club is reintroduced.

Right Arm Only Backswing Drill

The final key drill to use with the golfer to get a sense of the backswing movements and how simple they really are is the Right Arm Only Backswing Drill. This drill "presets" the right arm in the correct position without a club at first, and then has the golfer rotate

Figure 34 - The Right Arm Only Backswing Drill is a critical drill, especially for those who have been taught that swinging the golf club is dominated by the movements of the left arm and left side of the body.

to the proper position at the top.

In Figure 35, you can see a down the line view of this drill. In the image on the left, you can see the golfer has approximately 90 degrees of flexion, and the elbow is at about the base of the pec, indicating shoulder elevation has occurred. A slight amount of humeral rotation (discussed in the next section) can also be added while performing this drill. Once the right arm has been preset in this fashion, the golfer simply performs the shoulder blade glide to initiate rotation to the top. The key element here is that the right arm doesn't change position. It must not fly away from the body at the top, and the right humerus should be close to perpendicular to the chest. You will find right away that most students will let the arm drift away from the body while performing this drill and have their elbow pointing back behind them rather than parallel to the target line.

Once the golfer can perform this drill correctly, you may introduce the club and continue to work on the drill. Once the student can perform the movement with a club, have him bring the left hand up to support the club after making the full shoulder turn. This drill is a precursor to the extremely valuable "Throw the Ball Drill" that is covered in the downswing section, so it is important to fully understand this drill and be able to perform it flawlessly.

The Flying Right Elbow

Upon completion of this series of drills, some students may still encounter an improper folding of the right elbow and rotation of the right arm, commonly referred to as a flying right elbow. Examine the image in Figure 35 and take note of the position of the right elbow at the top of the backswing. Ideally, the right forearm is almost perpendicular to the ground. This ideal position can only be achieved if the right humerus is allowed to rotate clockwise during Move 2. In most cases, the right humeral rotation will occur naturally if the right arm is positioned correctly at setup, with the right elbow "pit" pointing away from the body, which represents NJA. If the student's

Figure 35 - Note the connection between the upper bicep and upper pec.

right elbow does not achieve this ideal position, the resulting swing plane can become very steep and will require multiple manipulations in the downswing to shallow out the angle of attack. Of equal importance to the swing plane is that when the elbow is allowed to move away from the body, the arms and hands move deep behind the body, making it likely that a better player will get stuck on the way down or a high handicap player will thrust his arms toward the ball from the top in a desperate effort to bring them back in front of the body. The last thing to note about the humeral rotation is that it also rotates the scapula clockwise, virtually "locking" it into a position that not only connects the golfer's arms to his core, but makes it nearly impossible to lift the arms too steeply or swing across the line at the top. While you may only address this issue with a handful of your better players in detail, it is vitally important that you understand the importance and ramifications of not properly rotating the humerus during the backswing.

Figure 36 - Humeral rotation keeps the club on plane and locks the scapula in a connected position at the top of the backswing, making it much easier to get the club back in front of the body during the downswing.

Diagnosing the Flying Right Elbow

The instructor must correctly diagnose the source of the improper folding of the right elbow in order to correct the issue and numerous swing faults it causes. First, check the right arm position at setup. Make certain the right elbow is pointing at the right hip at address. The "pit" of the elbow should point directly away from the golfer at setup, just as it does when standing in proper posture. Second, check at what point the right arm becomes disconnected from the body. The instructor should focus on the upper portion of the right bicep and the right pectoral muscle. This connection should be maintained throughout the backswing if the student remains in the box and proper shoulder elevation occurs rather than a pushing of the left arm across the chest. Quite often, the disconnection occurs due to the excessive arm swing during the early stages of the backswing, which manifests itself through a disconnection during Move 2. The right elbow folds behind the body, positioning the right forearm at an acute angle. A feeling that will assist the student is to imagine tossing a coin over the right shoulder (for a right-handed golfer) as the shoulders are turning in the backswing. To execute the toss, the right humerus rotates slightly clockwise, further pulling the right scapula into the box. The student should be aware of the right lat and right lower trapezius muscles engaging as the motion is performed correctly, and the connection will be maintained between the right upper bicep and right upper pectoral muscle (pectoralis major). The right elbow now will be in front of the right side of the torso and pointing towards the ground. The plane of the club will be flatter, and a shallower angle of attack is now possible without necessary manipulations in the downswing.

In summary, here is the sequence for the second half of the backswing:

- Right shoulder blade glide and obliques turn shoulders 45°. As they continue to pull, the hips are pulled around 45 additional degrees, creating a 90° shoulder turn.
- Arms remain straight and in front of the chest until right elbow flexion pulls the hands across center line.
- Shoulder elevation is happening primarily during Move 2.
- Right elbow flexion and humeral rotation occurs late in the backswing after Move 1 has been completed.

Looking at the Backswing Position - Down the Line

At the top of the swing, there are several key points that can be viewed and discussed. The first note is that the right arm is still in front of the upper torso. Depending on the golfer's build, the left arm may appear lower or higher than in the model above. This is dependent on how long the golfer's arms are in relation to his chest and how much shoulder elevation occurs during the

backswing, as well as how much flexibility the golfer has in the shoulder area, specifically the rear shoulder rotator cuff. It is preferable to avoid excessive shoulder elevation in order to reduce the amount the arms have to drop back down to get back in front of the body for impact.

When looking at the lower body, there are two key things to look for at this point. First, ensure that the hips have minimally rotated, as can be seen above. Second, you want to make sure the golfer's weight has moved to the center of the right ankle and is not over the balls of the feet or the outside of the foot. This can be seen above as the right knee is in NJA with the right ankle. Third, ensure that the knee flex of the right knee has been maintained from address so the right

glute can be powerfully engaged at the top of the swing.

Looking at the Backswing Position - Face On

At the top of the swing, a full shoulder turn with 45 degrees or more of separation from the hip turn is the typical look of the Rotary golfer. The weight will have clearly shifted to the right as can be seen in the image, and the left arm will be relatively straight. Ideally, for the sake of consistency, the left arm would be perfectly straight with the right arm at about 90 degrees of flexion. The reason for this is that adding any extra hinge to the left elbow introduces an unnecessary element of timing to the swing as the elbow will need to return to full flexion at impact in most cases. This is desirable for control at impact, and so you'll want to work to keep the arm straight throughout the swing.

The hands will typically appear slightly above the head as well when videoing with the camera set at waist height. This will vary from golfer to golfer depending on each one's build, but most will have this appearance because the arms must work up during the backswing in order to remain in front of the body and the steepness of the shoulder turn. If the hands appear below the head, check the golfer from down the line and ensure that he hasn't allowed the hands to drift back behind the body too far and that the right upper arm is still connected to the right pectoralis, as well as whether or not they've allowed their shoulders to rotate too flat.

Review questions:

1. What is responsible for turning the hips in the backswing?

2. What is responsible for creating a 90° shoulder turn in the backswing?

3. In which direction do the arms move throughout the course of the backswing?

4. Define the terms "Shoulder Elevation" and "Right Elbow Flexion."

5. What are three elements "Right Elbow Flexion" is responsible for in the backswing?

6. What is the correct sequence for initiation of "Shoulder Elevation" and "Right Elbow Flexion" in the backswing?

7. List the proper sequence for the entire backswing.

Chapter 10: The Downswing

In the entire golf swing, the downswing is probably the most misunderstood and misinterpreted move by amateur golfers. It must be understood that the downswing is the result of an uncoiling of the core muscles that were stretched during the backswing as well as a throwing motion of the right arm accompanied by a pulling with the left. Our initial goal in the downswing is to shift the weight back to the left and rotate the hips away from the target. The weight shift back to the left both creates momentum and puts the left hip in a stable and safe position to prepare for the upcoming rotation. It is critical that the golfer NOT perform this shift and rotation solely by pushing from the trailing leg. A pulling motion from the hip muscles that attach to the inner upper thigh will shift the weight fully back to the left while ensuring the golfer does not move past NJA. The rotation is also dominated by the left hip girdle. Doing so will rotate the hips fully to a 45 degree open position but not past. Only by pushing from the right leg will the golfer be able to move past this 45 degree open position. The key point that must be illustrated to the students is that the forces of movement in the downswing originate from the hips and obliques, resulting in a weight shift and a pulling to the left, NEVER from the upper body, shoulders, arms, etc.

The proper sequence of the downswing is as follows:

1. Externally rotate the left leg to move the knee directly over the left ankle.

2. Pull the weight over to the left with left hip adduction.

3. Plant the weight firmly by pushing the left ankle into the ground and activating the left glute.

4. Pull from the left oblique, turning the hips 45 degrees open in relation to the target line.

5. Pull with the left lat to pull the arms back in front of the torso.

6. Fire the right arm by extending from the right elbow, focusing the force through the right hand pressure points.

The result of this chain of events occurring in sequence and being performed from the proper origin is centripetal force: the hips rotating towards center and away from the target, and the arms and club are accelerated and move towards the target. In the image to the right, you can see that the hips have been rotated back away from the target, or to the left, while the club head works away from the body. For maximum club head speed, we want the hips rotating back to the left while

Figure 37 - The hips move in the opposite direction of the club head.

the upper torso remains passive. This can increase the separation between the upper and lower halves. The highest ball speeds are produced by golfers producing the maximal rotational separation between the upper torso and pelvis. Higher handicap golfers create significantly less separation and, thus, significantly less speed. Typically, amateurs only achieve approximately 35% of the separation of professionals. This separation can only occur when the downswing is performed in the proper sequence and from the correct origin of movement.

This entire sequence is initiated by the weight shift back to the left which starts with the external rotation of the left leg. Once the weight has been established firmly into the left side, the student should engage the left oblique muscle and pull the hips to the left. Pulling from the left oblique will turn the left hip away from the target, moving the hips a total of 90° from their position at the top of the backswing. To this point, the arms have worked back in front of the body by the downward pulling motion of the left arm and the pulling of the right pec. As the weight is transferred into the left side and hips are rotated 90°, the upper torso will be pulled around by this action and begin to be unwound by the hips. The result should be an impact position with the hips 45° open to the target line and the shoulders square to the target line. The weight is 80-90% on the left side, more specifically over the left ankle. The right heel should be off the ground by the time we reach the impact position as a result of this weight transfer and hip rotation, but only because it has been pulled up by the left side weight transfer and rotation, not because the golfer has pushed off the right in an effort to "spin" or slide the hips. Any student who has his right foot flat on the ground at impact has clearly not transferred enough weight to the left side or has a stance that is very narrow. This is quite common in students trying to master this move for the first time and is most typical of the higher handicappers. It is the Rotary Swing Instructor's job to determine the root cause of the weight remaining on the right side. Let us examine these causes in greater detail.

Common Causes of Hanging Back on the Right Foot

The first and most common cause occurs when the student attempts to rotate his hips before transferring his weight on to his left ankle. It is essential that the weight move over the left ankle, activating the left glute for stabilization, before the pulling with the left oblique occurs. If the weight transfer into the left ankle does not occur first in the downswing, when the student rotates his hips, he will be simply spinning out. The student will often be flat footed at impact

Figure 38 - A severe hang back like this one will result in fat and topped shots.

with the left hip being shy of NJA and will not get fully onto the left side until well after the golf ball is gone. The RST instructor must identify the issue and be able to illustrate to the student how to successfully transfer the weight into the left side before unwinding with the hips in the downswing.

Figure 39 - Here the golfer has pushed the left hip outside of neutral by shoving off the right foot, placing the hip in a vulnerable and weak position.

The second most common fault in the weight transfer occurs when the student attempts to rotate his hips and transfer his weight by pushing from the right side instead of pulling from the left. Pushing off the right foot most often creates a slide of the hips and moves the left hip past NJA, putting the golfer at serious risk for injury to the lead hip. The push also creates too much axis tilt (spine angle leaning away from the target when viewed from face on), leading to a path that is too far from the inside with hooks and blocks as the reward. The pushing motion is very common and also makes it hard for the golfer to keep his head behind the ball at impact. Only by using a pulling motion can we protect the hip from injury and be stacked over the golf ball for a powerful impact.

The RST instructor must be able to identify where the force of movement is coming from at the top of the downswing to identify the push from the right side as well as other common faults. By far, the most common mistakes made by students will involve the force of movement coming from the upper body, the shoulders, the arms, etc. to start the downswing. Any involvement of the upper torso in the downswing will destroy the sequence, path, plane and power. Force of movement coming from the upper body can be easily identified by the following:

- The right shoulder moves out towards the target line.
- The head moves in front of the ball.
- The plane of the club is now shifted into a steep, out to in attack angle and path.
- The shoulders will be open at impact.
- The weight gets transferred onto the balls of the feet.
- The student will most likely have trouble maintaining his original spine angle.

To the left is the image of the typical high handicap golfer who tries to heave his upper torso at the ball as his first move down rather than shifting the weight to the left, allowing the arms time to start working back down in front of the body. This is the epitome of the over the top slicer and can easily be rectified by having the student work and focus on the proper movements and stop focusing on striking the golf ball.

Impact and Address the Same?

One other example the RST instructor must be aware of is when the force of movement comes from the top, yet the student's shoulders are square at impact, accompanied by a noticeable lack of lower body rotation. The RST instructor will encounter this frequently in higher handicap golfers. The student in this situation has successfully rerouted the golf club by forcing his arms to drop by only using the arms to accelerate the golf club. The force of movement is still being provided by the upper torso, predominantly, the arms and hands, and the student will have a very flat footed appearance at impact and very little power. The student has effectively rerouted the golf club with his hands and arms but has not generated power from his core.

The student is simply relying on hand-eye coordination in order to strike the ball, which is a very inefficient and inconsistent manipulation and is not using the rotation of the hips to generate any speed. The impact and address positions should not be the same, so if you can't tell which frame you are looking at on video, there's a problem.

To summarize, the downswing is a powerful uncoiling motion, accompanied by a pulling down of the left arm while creating an underarm/sidearm throwing

Figure 40 - Am I at impact or address here? Who knows?!

motion with the right arm. We simultaneously transfer our weight from our right ankle to our left ankle, activating our left glute. Once this left glute is activated for stabilization and our weight is pushed down into the ground via the left ankle, a pulling with the left oblique, resulting in hip rotation, allows us to use rotational instead of lateral forces. As a result of this pulling, the hips rotate away from the target while the arms and the club move towards the target. The force of movement must come from our left oblique pulling our hip behind us, never from the upper torso. The hips will move a total of 90° from the position at the top of the backswing to impact. In relationship to the target line, the hips will be 45° open and the shoulders will be square.

When the downswing is performed correctly:

- The weight transfers onto the left ankle.
- The student pulls from the left oblique in order to rotate the hips.
- The right shoulder appears to move vertically down towards the right foot at the start of the downswing rather than out toward the ball when viewed from down the line.
- Shoulders remain closed, and the student's head will appear to drop slightly in the more powerful strikers.
- The golfer may give the appearance of slightly squatting as the weight transfer occurs with the flex in the right knee staying the same or increasing from where it was at the top of the swing.
- The club can be seen bisecting the right forearm as the hands work past belt high when viewed DTL.
- The student will easily maintain the original spine angle from setup or even increase slightly.
- The right ankle will begin to be pulled off the ground and work toward the left as the hips rotate 45° open.
- The right arm will be nearly fully extended at impact.
- The shoulders will be square at the impact position.

In the image below, we can see just how far the left hip has moved halfway through Move 3 from where it was at the top of the swing. The hips, if viewed from down the line, would be slightly open to the target at this point, while it is clear that the shoulders have remained closed, allowing the arms time to work back in front of the chest. (Note that because this is a driver, the stance is wider than 2" outside of neutral. This is ok for the driver when wanting to increase the

Figure 41 - The shift back to the left is the first momentum generator in the downswing and is the key to an efficient kinematic sequence.

launch angle as this helps shallow out the angle of attack when combined with a slightly forward ball position. The driver is a specialty club and the only one that we want to catch slightly on the upswing when trying to achieve maximum distance. So modifications to the setup are acceptable.)

In the next photo, we get a down the line view at the moment just after impact. It is here that we can see the shoulders square to the target line, while the hips have rotated 45 degrees more than the shoulders. The arms are extended in front of the chest, and the right heel is slightly off the ground. Note the slack in the shirt on the right side, signifying side bend. This indicates the golfer remained "in the box" into impact without the right shoulder jutting out toward the ball and disconnecting from the core. This position is paramount for transferring forces and energy from the hips and core generated during the downswing to the arms, club and, eventually, the ball. If the right shoulder blade is allowed to protract early in the downswing as it so often does in amateurs, there will be little energy transfer from the rotating torso, and the musculature of the shoulder girdle will be all that can be used to generate speed.

Figure 42 - At impact, the right arm will be nearly at full extension, with the shoulders being square to the target line and the hips open.

To further understand how the scapular protraction creates power loss, imagine a boxer throwing a punch. If the boxer were to throw a punch with the scapula in an elevated and protracted position, as you can feel for yourself by shrugging your shoulders and trying to throw a punch, it wouldn't be very powerful. The scapula is the primary connection point to the large musculature in the torso to the arms. If the scapula is depressed, you can feel how more energy can be transferred from the body. A feeling of being able to apply momentum and force from the pivot of the hips and the mass of the upper torso is the same feeling we seek during the downswing.

The "Throw the Ball" Drill

Perhaps the most useful drill you will put into your arsenal to assist with the learning process of the weight shift, backswing and downswing components is the Throw the Ball Drill. This very simple drill, when done correctly, allows the golfer to perform nearly every single movement in the golf swing and practice them while developing a sense of speed. It is especially helpful in teaching golfers to properly shift their weight in the downswing. This correct weight shift is truly the crux of the golf swing, both in timing it and getting into the proper impact position via the weight shift. This drill, because it mimics a natural throwing motion that most have learned at some point in their lives, comes naturally and even easily for many golfers, especially the more athletically versed.

To start, have the golfer pick up a golf ball and place it on the index finger pressure point of the right hand. Then, have the golfer perform the Right Arm Only Backswing drill to get to the proper position at the top. From there, have the golfer feel as though the hips and shoulders remain closed to the target line while he throws the ball down the line at another ball on the ground where the golf ball would normally be at address. What you will find is that almost all golfers will naturally shift their weight, unwind their hips and end up in a perfectly balanced finish position when doing this. And, even though you instructed them to not unwind their shoulders and hips, they will have done so in an effort to generate speed in the throw. It is simply unnatural for someone to perform this drill and not shift the weight and unwind the hips correctly.

Right Arm Only Downswing Drill

This drill will truly test the golfer's kinesthetic awareness and proprioception, while helping them ingrain the necessary movements for speed in the downswing. I have used this drill to help countless golfers pick up 10 mph of club head speed with the driver in less than ten minutes, so its value cannot be overstated.

Simply put, this drill involves swinging the club with the right arm only. It should be started from the preset position of the Right Arm Only Backswing drill at first. The student should understand that the goal is not to see how far they can hit the ball with this drill. Rather, the goal is to create synchronization between the rotating body and swinging arms while teaching the student where the speed comes from in the downswing. You should always start the student out with the ball on the tee when hitting balls with this drill, although a ball is completely optional. The student should feel that the right arm is releasing past the body coming into impact rather than the right shoulder continuing to turn ahead of the arm. In fact, the right shoulder should be almost stationary at impact in order for the right arm to be allowed to fully release and reach maximum speed before impact. In Figure 43, you can see just how little the right shoulder has moved from the time the club is parallel to the ground until just after impact. This is a vital component to generating a feeling of effortless speed. Think of the right shoulder as the handle of a whip. When you want the end of the whip to accelerate, you don't keep moving the handle in the direction you wish to crack the tip. You stop it from moving so that all the energy created by moving the handle can be transmitted out toward the end. The same is true here. If the right shoulder keeps moving toward the target, the arms and club will fully release after impact has already occurred, which is useless. By keeping the right shoulder back, the club head is allowed to accelerate past with great speed, allowing physics to take over. For golfers who are very aggressive with the shoulders rotating through impact, they will feel like they are putting significantly less effort into impact – and they are. This will be difficult to trust at first because it

Figure 43 - Note from face on that the right shoulder appears nearly stationary through the hitting area to give the arms a chance to release past the body with great speed.

will feel slower to them. Of course, it's not. In fact, it's much faster when done correctly, but it's always a good idea to keep a Swing Speed Radar handy to help drive the point home for them.

Review questions:

1. What is the correct origin of movement to start the downswing?

2. Define the proper sequence for the downswing.

3. Which muscle is responsible for rotating the hips?

4. What are some of the common results if the origin of movement in ˙ the downswing is initiated by the upper body?

5. What are the proper positions of the hips/shoulders at impact?

Chapter 11: Impact

All of the work done to this point is simply to get the golfer into the proper impact position. But what is the proper impact position, and why? Let's start with the body first.

At the top of the backswing, the golfer should have on average 45 degrees of separation between his hip turn and shoulder turn. The better players will dynamically increase this during the transition to as much as 55 or even 60+ degrees. If we move primarily from the left hip and oblique in the downswing, we know that the hips will rotate open about 45 degrees which should leave the shoulders square to the target line at impact given the following conditions:

- The golfer didn't push off the right side.
- The golfer didn't try and drive the right side (specifically the right shoulder) of the torso into the ball.
- The arms successfully worked back down in front of the body during the downswing.
- The golfer didn't overuse the pulling motion from the left side.

What about the golfers who increased their separation to more than 45 degrees? Wouldn't their shoulders be closed at impact if the hips are only open 45 degrees? No. The reason is that this stretch is not maintained and the shoulders will be pulled into impact faster as the stretched obliques release their energy created by the Short Stretch Cycle (SSC). This allows the shoulders to unwind faster, but not because they are actively being unwound. Rather, as the muscles contract, the shoulders are pulled around more swiftly. Of course, in doing this, the arms must also move faster to keep up, increasing the potential club head speed even more. This is a major source of power in the golf swing that every long hitter employs.

So, with the hips open and the shoulders square, where are the arms? The main focal point for the arms would be the right arm because it is actively transmitting energy from the body to the club through the extension of the right arm and unhinging and uncocking of the right wrist. Because the right wrist hinges/cocks on an angle during the backswing, it is not doing exclusively one or the other, but both unhinging and uncocking simultaneously. At impact, the right arm is nearly at full extension. It is not fully extended because it would no longer be able to actively apply force, and the club head would have been fully released, making it difficult to control direction.

Figure 44 - The right arm does not reach full extension until after impact.

From face on, the left arm and club will form a nearly straight line but will not become perfectly aligned until the bottom of the swing arc is reached. With an iron, this will occur several inches in front of the ball. With a driver, this can occur after impact, at impact or even before depending on the launch angle that the golfer is trying to achieve. For the utmost control, the hands should be slightly ahead of the golf ball at impact with all clubs; though, the amount will vary depending on the desired shot shape and trajectory. The head should remain behind the ball and the left hip directly over the left ankle. This may create the appearance of the hips being slid out too far laterally, but rest assured, this is not the case. The hip socket where the pivot occurs is well inside the outside of the hip. Also, the femur actually angles in from the outside of the hip to the knee joint. This and the hip turn create the illusion the hip is forward of neutral, but if you draw a vertical line from the center of the ankle, you will see this is not the case.

Figure 45 - At impact, the club shaft is leaning toward the target and does not move into a straight line condition with the left arm until it reaches the bottom of the swing arc, which is the center of the left shoulder.

Figure 46 - With the driver, the ball position can be more forward to encourage a shallower to positive angle of attack, making the impact conditions of the left side more in line. Because of this, I am just shy of NJA on the left hip as I have also adjusted my stance to be slightly wider to encourage the shallower attack angle.

Review Questions

1. Should the shoulders be open, shut or square at impact?

2. Where should the weight be at impact?

3. At what point does the right arm become fully extended?

Chapter 12: The Follow-through

The final "move" in the Rotary Swing model is the follow-through. There is not much to control in this portion of the golf swing, as it is mostly reaction. There are some key components to which we must pay close attention. From the impact position, the hips move an additional 45° at the completion of the follow-through. Total hip rotation from the top of the backswing to the end of the follow-through is 135°. The spine angle should be maintained well after impact, and the head should simply swivel

Figure 45 - Down the line view of the release during Move 4. Note that the spine angle has been maintained long into the follow-through.

to the left in order to follow the flight of the golf ball. Our weight should be 90% on our left side, more specifically in the left ankle and toward the heel and the hands should be in the center of the chest.

The biggest hurdle for amateurs to overcome during this portion of the golf swing is to maintain their spine angle. Amateurs tend to lift their eyes in order to track the flight of the golf ball, and where the eyes go, the head will follow. This causes them to stand up through impact. Ideally, after impact the head is still looking down towards

Figure 46 - Face on view of the release during Move 4. Note the left hip in NJA with the left ankle and the head remaining down and back behind the ball while the arms are being allowed to release for maximum speed through the hitting area.

the original spot of the ball, and the spine angle established at address is maintained until the arms have reached the three o'clock

Figure 47 - The left hip is safely in neutral when viewed both down the line and face on. Because of the stresses placed on this area of the body through the downswing, it is crucial that it be in the proper position to prevent injury.

position. The weight is 80-90% onto the left ankle, and only a small portion of the inside of the right toe is on the ground at this point, a clear indicator that there is minimal weight on the right side. It is not until the final frame that the spine angle has become upright, the shaft is across the back of the neck, the head is level to the ground and only the toe of the right foot is on the ground. The left leg is in neutral joint alignment, as the left hip is directly over the left knee which is directly over the left ankle. It is very important for the instructor to ensure that at no time does the left knee get closer to the target than the hip and ankle joints. This left side breakdown can cause unwanted stress on the knee joint and lower back.

9-TO-3 DRILL (WITH 2ND BALL)

A drill that should be utilized by the instructor to help the student maintain the spine angle and correctly perform the head swivel through impact is the 9-to-3 drill. The student should take the normal setup and have a second golf ball placed in-line with the golf ball about to be struck, approximately two inches outside of it. This second ball will serve as the focal point after impact. The student should swing the club back until the club is parallel to the ground (i.e. the nine o'clock position). The student should now hit the golf ball and stop his swing in the follow-through when the club is parallel to the ground (i.e. the three o'clock position). At this point, the student's focus should still be on the second golf ball. The student should have maintained the original spine angle established at address, the hips should be rotated open approximately 45° from original setup position, the hands should be in the center of the chest, 80-90% of the weight should be on the left ankle, the left leg should be in neutral joint alignment and the right ankle should be coming up only slightly off the ground. This drill is a multifunctional drill and is excellent for teaching the takeaway, weight transfer and the follow-through while allowing the golfer to get the pleasure of hitting balls rather than just performing drills.

Figure 48 - The 9-3 drill (note the second ball is not in position here).

The RST instructor should focus on the balance of the student upon completion of Move 4, as this will serve as a significant indicator of the origin of movement of the weight transfer that occurs during the transition between the backswing and downswing. This final piece of the golf swing can be utilized as an excellent diagnostic tool for the educated instructor.

Review questions:

1. What are the main characteristics of the Follow-through?

2. What is the potential danger if the left knee is outside of neutral joint alignment in Move 4?

3. What is the biggest hurdle for students to overcome in Move 4?

Chapter 13: Ball Flight Laws

At the end of the day, the only thing that really matters is sending the ball toward the target with the proper flight. The RST is built around making this easier to do more consistently and powerfully, but the instructor must still understand the factors that control the flight of the ball, specifically as it applies to curvature.

For years, the "Ball Flight Laws" developed by Dr. Gary Wiren were the accepted standard for what determined flight shape. Put simply, they stated that the initial direction of the ball was 100% determined by path and the curvature of the ball was determined by clubface angle. With the advent of radar based launch monitors, it has been possible to understand the true dynamics of ball flight like never before and in this case, prove that the "Laws" developed by Wiren are incorrect. Trackman (www.trackman.dk), a leading launch monitor developer, proved that the initial ball flight was, in fact, determined primarily by clubface angle at impact. According to Trackman's data, 85% of the initial ball flight direction is controlled by clubface angle and only 15% path. This is due to the fact that the ball generally leaves at an angle around 90 degrees to the clubface (this can vary slightly depending on clubhead speed due to the ball compressing on the face).

This is critical for the instructor to understand as a golfer can be hitting shots that appear to fly very straight but have a relatively severe in to out path and try to fix the wrong thing if solely determining how to fix the swing based on ball flight and the outdated laws put forth by Wiren. Clubface control is key to being a good golfer and it is critical that you understand the relationship of clubface angle and ball flight in order to properly diagnose your student's swing flaws.

ROTARY SWING ADVISORY BOARD AND INSTRUCTORS

The following doctors, biomechanists and instructors make up the Rotary Swing team. All have worked together using their unique expertise and experience to help mold the Rotary Swing into what it is today: the only golf swing model based on how the body is designed to move, complete with the learning system that is built around how the brain actually learns new movement patterns.

Chuck Quinton

Chuck Quinton is the founder of the Rotary Swing methodology and the Teaching Professional at Castle Pines Golf Club in Colorado. He also founded the Rotary Swing Golf Academy in Orlando, FL where he teaches during the winter months. He is the author of *The Rotary Swing* golf instruction book that has sold thousands of copies world wide as well as the instructional DVD series, *Swing Plane Made Simple* and *Short Game Made Simple*. His instructional website, www.RotarySwing.com is one of the largest golf instruction sites on the internet today with over 8,000 visitors per day and is host to 200 instructional videos that Quinton has created, as well as over 100 articles he has written. He has been featured as a guest on ESPN Sports Radio numerous times, as well as numerous local radio shows around the country.

Apart from teaching full time, he also plays professionally and maintains a plus 4 handicap at Castle Pines Golf Club, former home of the PGA Tour's *International* event. He has helped thousands of students of all abilities, including winners on the PGA Tour, Nationwide Tour, European PGA Tour, LPGA Tour, Futures Tour, Hooters Tour, Gateway Tour and numerous other mini-tours. It is through his thousands of hours of tireless research, continuing instruction and hard work that his website site and the Rotary Swing have come about.

Jeffrey P. Broker, Ph.D

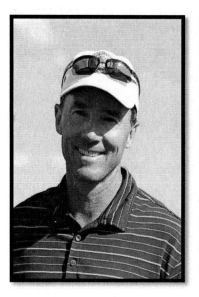

Dr. Broker is an Associate Professor in Biomechanics at the University of Colorado, Colorado Springs. He received his Bachelors degree in Mechanical Engineering at Cal Poly, San Luis Obispo in 1980, and a PhD in Biomechanics from UCLA in 1991. After obtaining his doctorate and prior to joining the University of Colorado, he spent eight years working as a Senior Biomechanist with the United States Olympic Committee.

He continues to work closely with Olympic Sports. Current sport biomechanics projects include the analysis of long and triple jump technique for the US National Track & Field Team; assessment of visual processing, perception and reaction for softball pitchers; cycling biomechanics/aerodynamics; injury mechanisms; and volleyball serve optimization. He also collaborates with local medical organizations in the area of clinical orthopedic biomechanics, injury mechanisms and musculoskeletal injury management.

Al Consoli

 Al Consoli is a native of Reading, Pennsylvania and is entering his seventh year in the golf business. Al was first introduced to the game by his grandfather at age 8 and has been playing for the better part of 26 years. Originally having the desire to seek a career as an osteopathic physician, he received a B.S. in Biology from American University in Washington D.C. He continued on to graduate school in a M.S. program for Basic Medical Sciences at New York Medical College and eventually attended medical school at Philadelphia College of Osteopathic Medicine. After successfully completing his first semester, Al decided to pursue his true passion in life, a career in golf. He immediately landed a job in New York at Sunningdale Country Club and has spent the better part of his career in the northeast United States, most recently as a Teaching Professional at Westchester Country Club in Rye, NY. Over the years, Al came to realize that the ability to create a consistent, repeatable golf swing lies in the true understanding of human

physiology and proper biomechanics. His journey led him to the Rotary Swing Golf Academy in April Of 2009. During his time with the RSGA, Al has spent countless hours learning the intricacies of the RST, co-authored this RST training manual and the accompanying certification examination, filmed several popular instructional videos, lectured in the RST online seminars and coached countless students, both at our teaching facility in Florida and through our online lesson program. Al is the lead instructor at the Rotary Swing Golf Academy in Orlando, FL.

Glossary

Anterior: situated before or at the front of.

Ball-and-socket joint (Hip Joint): the type of joint with the greatest range of motion, a full 360 degrees. Therefore, it is imperative that the hip joint be the primary rotating joint in a rotary-powered swing and not a hinge joint like the knee.

Box: a term coined by Alison Thietje used to describe the core of the body, both anteriorly and posteriorly, including abdominals, obliques, trapezius (middle and lower fibers only) and lats; students will feel these muscles engage when they depress their shoulders.

Deltoid: the large, thick, triangular muscle that gives the rounded outline to the shoulder. It surrounds the shoulder joint and raises the arm away from the body to the front, side and rear.

External Oblique Abdominal: situated on the side for part of the abdomen, it helps flex and rotate the trunk.

Extension: the act of straightening a limb.

External Hip Rotation: at the hip joint, turning the leg outwardly from the midline of the body.

Flexion: the act of flexing or bending a limb.

Gemellus Inferior: muscle that rests on the back part of the hip joint. Rotates and stabilizes the hip.

Gemellus Superior: muscle that rests on the back part of the hip joint, and is the smaller of the two. Rotates and stabilizes the hip.

Gluteus Maximus: the most superficial muscle in the gluteal region, it is a very broad and thick fleshy mass. Its large size is one of the most characteristic points in the muscular system in man, connected as it is with the power he has of maintaining the trunk in the erect posture. It helps to stabilize the hip.

Hinge Joint (Knee Joint): a joint that allows motion in only one plane.

Internal Oblique Abdominal: located just underneath the external oblique, it helps flex and rotate the trunk.

Internal Obturator: a muscle situated partly within the cavity of the pelvis and partly at the back of the hip joint. It rotates and stabilizes the hip.

Intervertebral Disc: a disc of composite structure interposed between the adjacent surfaces of the bodies of the vertebrae, forming the chief bond of connection between these bones.

Joint: the place of the union, usually more or less movable, between two or more bones.

Kinesthetic: the sensation of movement or strain in muscles, tendons and joints; muscle sense.

Kinetic Chain: In this manual, referring to an ordered sequence of body segment movement (i.e. glutes activate, hips rotate, shoulders rotate, right arm extends, etc.) with the goal of maximizing club head speed at impact.

Kyphosis: a deformity of the spine characterized by extensive flexion; hump-backed.

Latissimus Dorsi: the broad flat muscle, which covers the mid and lower half of the back. This muscle is one of the focal points in the Rotary Swing, as it is the primary muscle we focus on to keep a student in the box. It covers the largest surface area of any muscle in the body, and it rotates and lowers the arm.

Lordosis: An abnormal forward curvature of the spine in the lumbar region.

Neutral Joint Alignment: refers to when the joints are in their neutral positions. Imagine a straight line from the center of the ear hole down the center of the shoulder and hip joints, behind the knee joint and through the center of the ankle joint. This is neutral joint alignment and the way the body was designed to carry itself. When describing neutral joint alignment on the lower half of the body from the anterior view, imagine a line from the center of the hip joint through the center of the knee joint and the center of the ankle joint. Neutral joint alignment can be used to describe any relationship in which a straight line may be drawn between various joints.

Neuromuscular Reeducation: the definition given to any form of athletic training, rehabilitation program or bodily movement that requires your muscles and nerves to learn or relearn a certain behavior or specific sequence of movements. Learning to ride a bicycle is a good example of how your muscles and nerves eventually learn and develop the neural networks and motor pathways necessary to ride effectively. Initially, you start off with training wheels. Your body begins to develop a broad kinesthetic sense (sensation of muscle movements through nerves) necessary to maintain your balance. Shortly afterwards, one training wheel is removed, and your muscles and nerves are forced to increase their kinesthetic ability or awareness to maintain a tighter balance. Ultimately, both training wheels are removed, and all of your muscles and nerves become perfectly coordinated together producing the desired effect, riding the bike. Athletes who train to excel in a given sport subject themselves to a higher level of reeducation all the time. Every day in practice, your muscles are constantly refining the pathways necessary to master these movements, making them appear effortless and without any conscious thought. Studies show it takes approximately 3000 to 5000 repetitions in order to perform a sequence of movements correctly without conscious thought; in other words, for it become a habit.

Pectoralis Major: a broad, thick, muscle of the upper chest. It draws the arm in toward the body and rotates the upper arm inward.

Posterior: situated behind or at the rear of.

Proprioception: The unconscious perception of movement and spatial orientation arising from stimuli within the body itself.

Protraction: In this manual, typically referring to the movement of the shoulder blades up and away from the spine.

Pyriformis: a flat muscle that is situated partly within the pelvis at its posterior part, and partly at the back of the hip joint. It rotates and stabilizes the hip.

Quadrates Femoris: a short, flat muscle located in the hip region. It rotates and stabilizes the hip.

Rectangle: a term coined by Alison Thietje to describe the uppermost region of the torso, namely the deltoids, the upper pectoralis major and upper fibers of the trapezius. These muscles become engaged when the student shrugs the shoulders and gets out of the box.

Rectus Abdominis: a long, flat muscle that extends along the whole length of the front of the abdomen. It flexes the spine and draws the pelvis forward.

Retraction: In this manual, typically referring to the movement or position of the shoulder blades down and in toward the spine.

Rotation: the turning or movement of a body around its axis.

Scapula: the shoulder blade.

Sternocleidomastoid: a large, thick muscle, which passes obliquely across the side of the neck. It is responsible for tilting and twisting the neck.

Trapezius: a broad, flat, triangular muscle which covers the upper and back part of the neck and shoulders and extends down into the mid back. It contains upper, middle and lower fibers, each of which must be understood. The upper fibers elevate the scapula, causing a shrugging motion of the shoulders. The middle fibers retract the scapula, drawing it towards the body's midline. The lower fibers depress the scapula, drawing it inferiorly. This and the rhomboid are truly the muscles responsible for moving the scapula, but many students are not fully aware of this muscle when it is engaged. We instead talk about feeling the larger lat muscle engaged as it is easier to feel and if the shoulder blade is elevated, this activation of the lat will be lost. It is important to understand we are describing the feel, but the trapezius and rhomboid are responsible for scapular movement.

References used for the glossary:

www.dictionary.com

www.wikipedia.org

medical-dictionary.thefreedictionary.com

Acknowledgements

Special thanks to Alison Thietje who coined some of the terminology used in the Rotary Swing Tour methodology and who encouraged us to look at the golf swing from a completely objective medical and anatomical perspective. Also, special thanks go out to the online members of the RotarySwing.com website whose ongoing support of our efforts have allowed us to develop the Rotary Swing into what it is today. Last, but certainly not least, thanks to Josh Eaton who is the best and most detail oriented editor I've ever worked with!